MAKE CLOTH DOLLS

A Foolproof Way to Sew Fabric Friends

Terese Cato

C&T PUBLISHING

Text copyright © 2010 by Terese Cato

Artwork copyright © 2010 by C&T Publishing, Inc.

PUBLISHER: Amy Marson

CREATIVE DIRECTOR: Gailen Runge

ACQUISITIONS EDITOR: Susanne Woods

EDITOR: Liz Aneloski

TECHNICAL EDITOR: Ann Haley

COPYEDITOR/PROOFREADER: Wordfirm Inc.

COVER DESIGNER: Kristy Zacharias

BOOK DESIGNER: Rose Sheifer-Wright

PRODUCTION COORDINATOR: Kirstie L. Pettersen

PRODUCTION EDITOR: Julia Cianci

ILLUSTRATOR: Mary Flynn

Photography by Christina Carty-Francis and Diane Pedersen of C&T Publishing, Inc., unless otherwise noted

Published by C&T Publishing, Inc., P.O. Box 1456, Lafayette, CA 94549

Library of Congress Cataloging-in-Publication Data

Cato, Terese.

  Make cloth dolls : a foolproof way to sew fabric friends / Terese Cato.

     p. cm.

ISBN 978-1-57120-962-7 (soft cover)

1. Dollmaking. 2. Soft toy making--Patterns. I. Title.

TT175.C393 2010

745.592'4--dc22

                              2010001672

Printed in China

10 9 8 7 6 5 4 3 2 1

Dedication

In memory of Aunt Marie

Acknowledgments

I would like to thank C&T Publishing for allowing me the opportunity to reach beyond the students in my workshops and share my love for sewing. Being able to teach something that you love is truly a blessing.

Thank you to my husband for his patience and understanding. His unending support means everything to me.

CONTENTS

Preface

When I teach a doll workshop, I encourage the participants to make choices that appeal to them and let their dolls evolve. Most people begin by saying that they want their doll to look exactly like the project doll. Then funny things start to happen. They choose the fabrics that they like. The younger a person is, the younger his or her doll appears to be, and the older the person is, the older the doll appears to be. No two faces look alike, and none of them are a carbon copy of the project doll. By the time people get to the hairstyle, they find themselves wanting it to be different from the project doll's because another choice of hairstyle just seems to fit better. By the end of the class, there are no two dolls that look the same. They may have the same body and use the same pattern for the clothes, but that is where the similarities end. What is funniest to me is how the doll starts to resemble the doll maker in some way. The best part is hearing how everyone enjoyed the process so much, and hearing people begin to talk about how they're going to make the next doll.

Let your own creativity take over. Take your time to learn the basic body construction. When the body is done it is a blank canvas ready for your own creative ideas. Sometimes when I start a doll, I have a complete, finished picture of her in my head. I know exactly where I'm going, and it just flows right out. Then there are times when I think I know where I'm going, but the doll just demands that I make changes to my original plan. Either way, I'm always happy with the end result. If you have a sewing machine with a bunch of fancy stitches that you've never tried, now is your chance. Use coordinating threads to stitch on the edges of sleeves, skirts, pants, aprons—anywhere you see a place to add some detail.

Just remember that there are no mistakes, just happy accidents. If you want to put sandals on your doll to show off her beautifully sculpted and painted toes, but her feet turn out to be less than you expected, put closed shoes on her instead. There is only one doll on whose face I intentionally put a mole. All the other moles were placed there to cover up a slip with the pencil.

I remember the first time I took my husband to an art and craft show. He is a man's man—all about sports. He has taken on the difficult task of teaching me the rules of all the games. I have shown him the work and love that go into handmade items. As we were driving to the show, he asked me what we were going to buy. I explained that if something "spoke to me" then I would buy it. As only a wife can read her husband's face, I knew he was thinking, "Oh boy! This is going to be a great afternoon." As we walked around, he began to comment on the amount of time and work that some of these people obviously put into their craft. Then it came. The moment something spoke to me. An artist who was a welder by trade created beautiful home décor and accents—in this case, an old-fashioned sled with iron runners that came up the front and turned into geese. It was tall enough to use as a bench or coffee table, and I began to examine it closely as I tried to envision where I'd place it in our home. As my husband watched me, he asked if it was speaking to me. He then began to examine it more closely himself and announced that he thought it might be speaking to him also. The sled is proudly displayed in our foyer and is quite a conversation piece.

I often hear that my dolls speak to people. The dolls tell a story or have an attitude that draws people to them. Sometimes a doll reminds them of someone they know or even of themselves. The details stand out and show the care and time that were taken to create this character. If the doll makes people smile or laugh, then they know they have to have one.

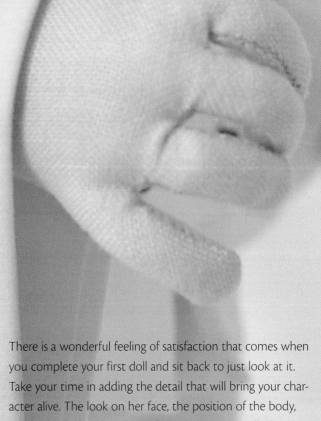

There is a wonderful feeling of satisfaction that comes when you complete your first doll and sit back to just look at it. Take your time in adding the detail that will bring your character alive. The look on her face, the position of the body, the fabric choices for the outfit, and the props will all come together to help tell her story without explanation. Use these elements to give your doll a personality and an attitude. When you are all done and sitting back to admire your handiwork, she will tell you what her name is. Name your doll, and then you can fill in the blanks to tell the rest of her story.

When people point at your doll and laugh or chuckle, take it as a compliment. It simply means that she spoke to them, and they understood.

Introduction

If you have been sewing for a while, you will most certainly have a drawer full of tools to use. If you are a beginner, you really need only the essential equipment to start. When you want to try something new, there's nothing more discouraging than a long list of tools you don't have. If you have stuffing tools, by all means use them, but if you don't, a pencil or a chopstick works just as well. There are three tools that are "musts" to help you achieve the best results: tiny turning tubes, extra-long doll-making needles, and watercolor pencils.

General Sewing Equipment

Sewing machine

Straight pins

Sharp scissors for cutting fabric

Tape measure

All-purpose sewing thread

Quilting thread for attaching body parts and face sculpting

Seam ripper

Needles for hand sewing, including curved needles and 5″ and 7″ doll-making needles

Safety pins for threading elastic (or a bodkin if you have one)

Iron for pressing doll clothes

General Doll-Making Equipment

Mechanical pencil for tracing templates on fabric

Reverse-action tweezers or hemostats for turning body parts and making fingers (Reverse-action tweezers can be found in the scrapbooking tools department of your craft store or online.)

Stuffing tool: unsharpened pencil, chopstick, or dowel (or stuffing tool of your choice)

Water-soluble marker to mark face for sculpting

Wire cutter to cut pipe cleaners for fingers

Pliers to bend over ends of pipe cleaners

Tiny turning tubes for turning fingers (A set of several small sizes is available through my website, www.teresecato.com.)

White craft glue for assembling props

Embroidery thread for doll faces

Watercolor pencils (These can be found in the art section by the box or individually.)

Paintbrushes 2 stiff, blunt paintbrushes for blending watercolor pencils on fabric: a larger one for wetting the fabric and blending the cheek color, and a smaller one to blend the colors of the eyes and lips

Hand Sewing Stitches

A ladder stitch is used to sew the stuffing holes closed and to attach the head and limbs. It is also used to close openings in the clothes of the doll. This stitch is also known as an invisible stitch.

Ladder stitch with loose stitches (When the thread is pulled tight, the stitches will disappear, leaving a neat seam.)

A couching stitch is an embroidery stitch used to outline or accent a design. Usually, many couching stitches are used in a row. When sculpting the doll face, we will use one couching stitch at a time to hold the nose-wing thread and the mouth thread in place.

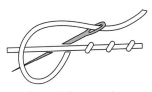

Couching stitch

The whipstitch is used to hand sew the shoes and purses. Line up the fabric edges with wrong sides together. The needle goes in the bottom of the fabric and comes out the top of the fabric. Pull the thread through both of the fabric layers. Carry the thread over the top of the work, insert the needle in the back of the fabric, and come out the top again. Keep the stitches an even distance from the edge of the fabric for a neat look.

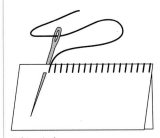

Whipstitch

If you want the stitches on the shoes to stand out, use a blanket stitch. Choose a contrasting thread color to make the stitching pop. The blanket stitch is done the same as the whipstitch except that the thread is drawn through the loop before it is pulled tight.

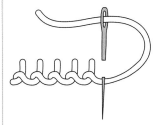

Blanket stitch

Some of the clothes on the dolls call for a gathering stitch. The gathering stitch is used on the top edge of a sleeve or the waist of a skirt, for example. If you sew with your machine on the longest stitch length, you will be able to pull the end of the thread and gather the fabric.

Gathering stitch

A Final Word Before You Begin

Whatever project you make, it is always a good idea to read through the directions before you begin. I spoke to someone who had bought one of my patterns. She was so excited to make the doll. She bought all the fabric, cut everything out, and then opened the directions. The very first line said, *"Please read through the entire pattern directions before you begin."* Then she read, *"Trace, sew, and then cut out."* Eliminate the element of surprise, and read the directions first.

All the seam allowances in the patterns are ¼" unless otherwise stated. Whether you are sewing body parts or clothes, backstitch at the beginning and end of each seam. This will lock the stitches in and keep the seam from pulling open. It is a good idea to have the iron out as you are sewing the clothes. Press the seams open as you sew. Do not press open the seams of the body parts.

Most importantly, have fun, let your creativity take over, and enjoy the process.

CHAPTER ONE

The Cloth Doll:
Basic Body Construction

Doll or Toy?

The most difficult decision will be deciding which doll to make first. Most of the dolls I make are for adults, so the sky is the limit with embellishing. I love the tiny buttons and the jewelry with beads and charms. It is fun to create all the props for the dolls to hold, and it helps turn them into characters with a story. The patterns in this book are **not intended for young children**. All the details that make the dolls so special are not safe for children to play with. Any toy that you make for a child needs to be age appropriate.

My two-year-old granddaughter, Emma, comes into my work-room and reaches up toward the dolls high on the shelf with a wild look of excitement on her face. Sadly for her, they are not safe for her to play with.

If you make dolls and have young girls in your life, they will undoubtedly be asking for one. If you make a doll that will be a toy for a young child, you will need to make it simply, without all the tiny buttons and embellishments, so it will be safe for young hands. Children tend to put things in their mouths, so exclude any of the embellishments that could be swallowed.

I do not recommend putting wire in the fingers of a doll that is intended for a child. I would make mitten-shaped hands filled with stuffing only, a fabric body with a painted face, a simple dress without buttons and embellishments, and hair made of yarn or ribbon. A young child will be just as happy with a simply made doll, and you will know it is safe for little hands to love. You are putting a lot of time and love into creating a doll for a special little girl, but you need to understand that the doll will never again look as good as it did the day you presented it to her.

The Basics

This chapter is a basic guide to constructing the doll body. You should read through this chapter before working with any of the patterns in this book. As you work with the patterns, you can refer back to this chapter for additional detailed instructions.

You can change the shape of the body or the position of the arms and legs, but the basic construction will remain the same. The chapters that follow will show you how to take these skills and create your own character. There are no limits to your options.

Abby, the standing doll (Chapter 2, page 32); Estelle, the sitting doll (Chapter 3, page 49); and Jilly, the cross-legged doll (Chapter 4, page 60) are all the same 16″ scale. You can follow the pattern for a project's particular body, or mix and match the body pieces, hairstyles, and clothes to create your own character. Each of these three dolls offers a different head shape and leg and arm positions. Choose one color of body fabric to work with so everything will match if you decide to mix things up. Emily Ann, the 22″ rag doll (Chapter 5, page 70) is a different scale and not interchangeable with the 16″ doll patterns in this book.

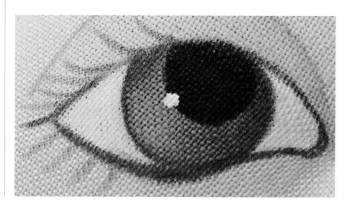

Abby

Jilly

Estelle

Emily Ann

Steps to Create the Doll Body (Overview)

1. Devise a plan. Decide whether your doll will be sitting or standing, and choose the pattern and the templates.

2. Choose the fabric to be used for the body. Trace the body templates on the fabric, following the directions of the pattern you chose.

3. Sew the body pieces carefully on the traced lines. Notice that the patterns show dashed lines for sewing and solid lines for cutting.

4. Cut out the body pieces with a ⅛" seam allowance for the sewing lines and cut directly on the solid lines that you did not sew.

5. Turn the body pieces right side out, stuff them, and then sew the stuffing holes closed.

6. Attach the arms and legs. If it's in your plan to paint the fingers and toes, do it before you attach the limbs.

7. Sculpt and paint the face.

8. Create an outfit and dress the doll.

9. Sew the head to the body. Attach the hair to the head.

10. Embellish with jewelry, props for the hands, or whatever fits with the theme of your doll.

Choosing the Fabric

All the doll bodies in this book are made with Kona Cotton fabric by Robert Kaufman Fabrics. You can find it at most fabric and quilt shops. It comes in many solid colors suitable for bodies, ranging from white to dark browns. I suggest that you start with the Kona Cotton, and then once you are comfortable with the techniques, you can experiment with other fabrics. If you do a search on the Internet for doll fabric, you will find lots of wonderful fabrics, but you may find them to be more expensive than the Kona Cotton. Kona Cotton is easy to find locally, and because it is relatively inexpensive, you can experiment to your heart's content. You can find other fabrics of a similar weight and thread count that will also work well. Muslin and broadcloth are not stable enough because of their light weight and lower thread count.

When it comes to dressing your doll, there are endless possibilities for fabric. If you are a beginner, you will find that cotton fabrics are easy to work with. Most of the clothing items are small and don't require much fabric. If you sew and have a fabric stash, you can search there first. Another really great place to find fabric is the discount bin at the fabric store. Often you will find odd fabrics that no one wants, and they will be just the thing you're searching for. One important thing to keep in mind when choosing a print fabric is the scale of the print. Smaller prints will help keep things in proportion, and the end result will be more pleasing.

When I make a doll, I choose fabrics for the clothes in much the same way a quilter chooses fabrics for a quilt. I decide what my color palette is, and then I stack coordinating fabrics until I'm happy with the selection. It's fun to mix several prints together, and as long as they complement each other, they look great. Several print fabrics will look good together if they have something in common, such as color, to pull them together. As you try grouping different fabrics, keep a few things in mind.

■ Begin with a print fabric that includes two or more colors. Try grouping fabrics that have at least one color in common.

- Vary the density and the size of the prints. Choose a small-, medium-, and large-scale print (in scale or proportion with the size of the doll) in the fabric grouping.

- Then, finally, mix the color value. Color value is the relative lightness or darkness of a color. Several fabrics with the same color value will blend together as one. The contrast of a light, medium, and dark will help separate the fabrics.

All these things will come together to create a grouping that is pleasing to the eye. When choosing a white or off-white for pantaloons and underwear, choose a white-on-white print for more interest.

If you choose too many solid colors, you may find that your end result seems flat. If you look closely, you will notice that (with the exception of Chef Caesar) there is not a solid-color fabric used for any of the doll clothes in this book. You may not wear a flowered blouse with striped pants, but it might just be the thing that pulls your doll's outfit together.

Making the Body

Making and Laying Out the Body Templates

1. Photocopy the proper template patterns for your doll. Template patterns appear on pages 96–110.

Using a photocopy machine will give you more accurate templates than if you trace them. The template patterns also have useful information and directions that will be needed as you work with them. I recommend photocopying the template patterns onto cardstock and then cutting them out to make templates. Templates made of cardstock will last longer and are easier to trace on the fabric than are plain-paper templates.

2. Use a pencil to draw an arrow in the direction of the straight-grain stretch (see Note, page 14), on the edge of the fabric. Lay out the legs, arms, body, and head templates, matching the direction of the arrows on the templates with the arrow you drew on the fabric.

TIP

If you lay out the head with the direction of the straight-grain stretch going from side to side, the face will be wide, with full cheeks. If the direction of stretch goes from forehead to chin, the face will be longer. Experiment with the head for different shapes.

NOTE

The term "straight grain" can be confusing. You may know that the straight grain is parallel to the selvage edge of the fabric, but the problem is that if you use scrap fabric, you may not know which edge is the selvage. Instead, simply find the direction of the straight-grain stretch in the fabric (not the diagonal bias). We don't tend to think of cotton fabrics as having any stretch, but one direction will have more give in it than the other. The one with more give is the straight grain.

With your fingers, pull the fabric parallel with the selvage edge (the selvage edge usually has the name of the fabric printed on it) and then pull the fabric parallel with the cut edge. If you don't know which edge is which, look closely at the fabric to determine the direction of the weave. Pull the fabric along the weave first in one direction and then the other. Even if it is slight, one direction will have more stretch than the other.

Tracing the Body Templates

1. Fold the fabric with the right sides together.

When working with solid colors, it can often be very difficult to determine the right side of the fabric from the wrong side. When fabric is wrapped on the bolt, it is folded with the right side out. If you are using a piece of fabric from the scrap bin and you are uncertain how it came off the bolt, make a good guess and use that side consistently as the right side.

IMPORTANT

*The body templates will be traced onto the fabric, sewn, and **then** cut out.*

This may be a new technique for you, since most patterns tell you to cut out the pattern pieces and then sew them together. It is easier and will result in a much neater job if you sew first and then cut out.

I recommend using a mechanical pencil to trace the templates on the fabric, since it will give you a thin line to sew directly on. A #2 pencil or a fabric marker will result in a thicker line. Make the pencil lines just dark enough to be seen. If the lines are too dark, they may show through light-colored fabric.

When it comes to sewing the fingers, you need to be as precise as possible because they are small and close together.

2. Carefully trace each template and then pin the fabric together.

Sewing the Body

The stitch length on your sewing machine should be set very short—1.5 to 2, depending on your machine (the perfect-size stitch will give you 2 stitches between the fingers and 4 stitches across the fingertips; see page 16).

Notice that the templates show dashed lines for *sewing lines* and solid lines for *cutting lines*.

1. Sew around the leg and body pieces only on the dashed lines. Sew slowly. Wait until instructed to sew around the arm/hand and head pieces.

If you can't keep your stitches on the pencil line, you are sewing too fast. Use a clear or open presser foot if you are having trouble seeing the pencil line.

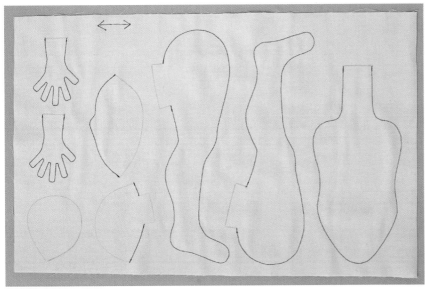

Stitch on the dashed lines. Example sewn with red thread for clarity only.

2. Check the seams. If the sewing line isn't smooth or you've sewn off the line, fix it, because it won't get better once you turn the piece right side out.

Stuffing the Body and Legs

I must admit that I don't use any fancy tools made specifically for stuffing dolls. A wooden dowel, a new unsharpened pencil with a clean eraser, or a chopstick is my tool of choice. Try a few different things and use what works best for you. Use a stuffing tool if you have one, but don't buy one before trying what you already have on hand.

I use polyester fiberfill for stuffing my dolls. There are a few brands that work well. Don't use stuffing that looks and feels like cotton balls. It tends to look lumpy and bumpy under the fabric.

Stuff the body and leg pieces firmly, but not so firmly that the seams appear to be stressed.

Use a pencil (or your stuffing tool of choice) to pack down the stuffing as you go. The ankles and neck tend to get a wrinkle and bend in them if they are not stuffed firmly enough. Once the body is stuffed, it is very difficult to fix this problem, so pay attention to these areas as you stuff.

Refer to the specific project instructions to attach the legs.

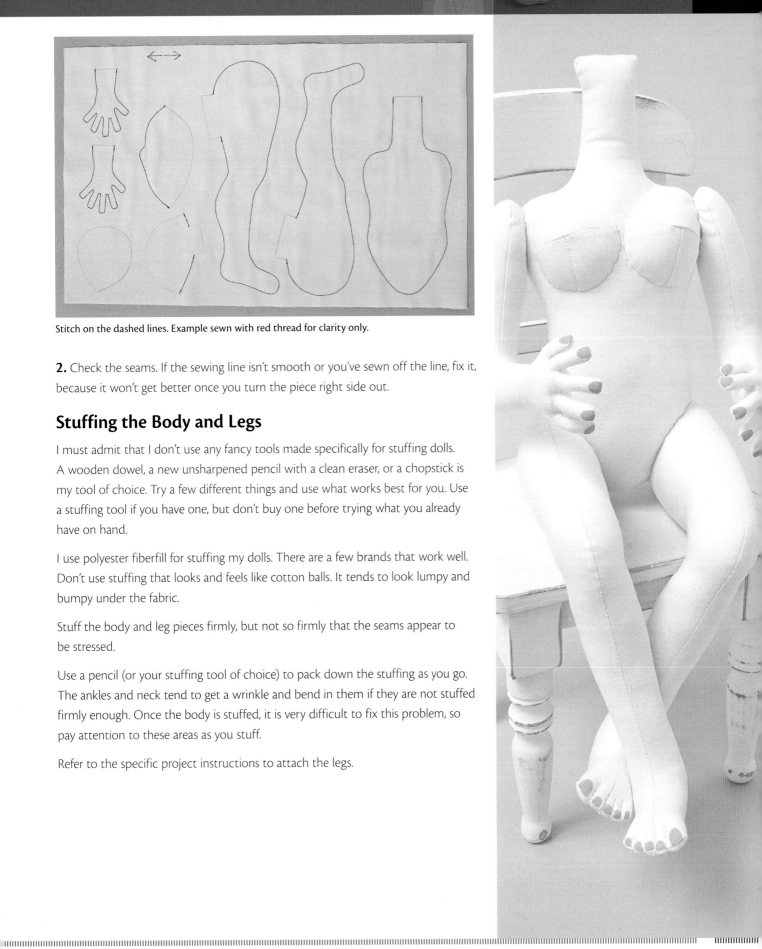

Perfect Fingers Every Time

All the dolls in this book use this same technique to wire the fingers.

I can't stress enough how important it is to take your time with the details. It is the attention to detail that will make your doll truly special.

The question I get asked the most is, "How do you get the fingers so perfect?" When I teach a doll workshop and take the participants through the steps, they are surprisingly pleased with their dolls' *perfect fingers*. So take your time and go through the process step by step, and everyone will ask you how you got the fingers so perfect.

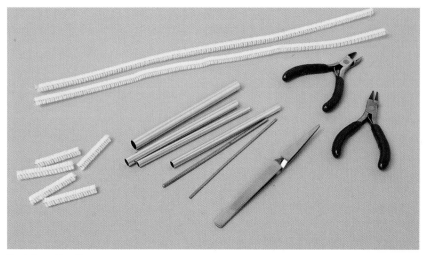

Tools for wiring fingers

It doesn't matter if you are making just the hands, or the arms and hands in one piece—the steps are the same. The materials needed are white pipe cleaners and stuffing. Use only white pipe cleaners because colored ones may show through the fabric. Use wire cutters or old scissors to cut the pipe cleaners, not your sharp fabric scissors. The tools needed are turning tubes and reverse-action tweezers (they open when you squeeze them) or hemostats.

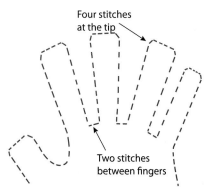

Four stitches at the tip

Two stitches between fingers

Sew same number of stitches across tip of each finger.

SEWING THE ARM/HAND PIECES

1. Set your sewing machine to the smallest stitch length.

2. Sew on the dashed seamline.

Slow down when you come to the fingers. Use the wheel on your sewing machine to hand sew 1 stitch at a time around the tip of each finger. As you sew around the first fingertip, count the stitches. If you have 4 stitches across the fingertip, sew 4 stitches across the other fingertips. This will give you more uniform fingers—otherwise they may all have a different shape.

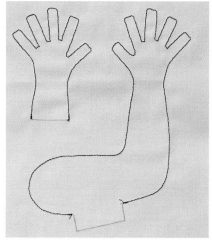

Stitch hands.

If you can fit 2 stitches between each finger, then your stitch is small enough. If you take it slow, you will be able to stay on the stitched line. If you are having trouble seeing the needle, try a clear or open presser foot on your machine. If you can't stay on the line, you are sewing too fast. If you wander off the line, stop and go back. If you don't fix it now, it will only look worse when you turn the fingers right side out.

CUTTING OUT THE ARM/ HAND PIECES

Cut out the arms/hands with a ⅛" seam allowance. Cut straight down between the fingers, being careful not to cut the stitches between the fingers. Using a fabric like Kona Cotton for the body is important because it has a high thread count and is much thicker than a fabric like muslin. The more threads the tiny stitches have to hold onto, the less the chance the seam will rip out.

TURNING THE ARM/HAND PIECES RIGHT SIDE OUT

Once you try using the turning tubes, you'll be hooked because they make quick work of turning fingers, as well as other body parts and small clothing items, such as belts and hair ties. Turning tiny fingers without turning tubes can be a slow and frustrating process that may leave you with disappointing results. This tool is a must-have for perfect fingers every time.

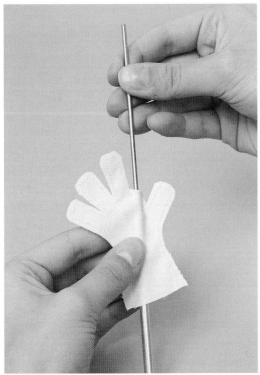

Use turning tube.

Turning tubes come in sets with several sizes. The set will include an open pipe and a solid rod. The open pipe slides inside the hand and up into the finger, all the way to the tip.

1. Choose a pipe size that fits snugly into the finger without putting too much stress on the seams. Choose the solid rod that fits best into the pipe.

The solid rod is pushed into the pipe, while the other end of the pipe is on the table to give a solid footing to push against.

2. Fold over the seam allowance at the fingertip so the rod is pushing on more than one thickness of fabric. Push the finger into the pipe. Pull the pipe out. The finger will be turned and inside the palm of the hand.

If you are having trouble pushing the rod into the pipe, you may need to try a larger pipe.

3. Repeat with all the fingers. The fingers will all be turned inside the palm of the hand.

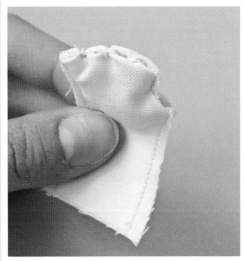

All fingers are turned into palm of hand.

4. Turn the arm right side out and reach into the palm of the hand with tweezers or a hemostat and gently pull the fingers right side out.

WIRING THE FINGERS

1. Cut the white pipe cleaners to a length that will reach from the fingertip to the middle of the palm of the hand (about 1½″ for a 22″ doll and 1¼″ for a 16″ doll).

2. Fold over the wire at each end of the pipe cleaner with pliers, so the sharp ends don't poke through the fabric. Run your finger across the ends to check for sharp edges.

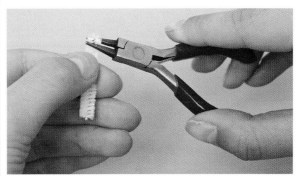

Fold over ends of pipe cleaners.

3. Use reverse-action tweezers to guide a prepared pipe cleaner into a finger, pushing it all the way to the fingertip. Part of the pipe cleaner will extend into the palm.

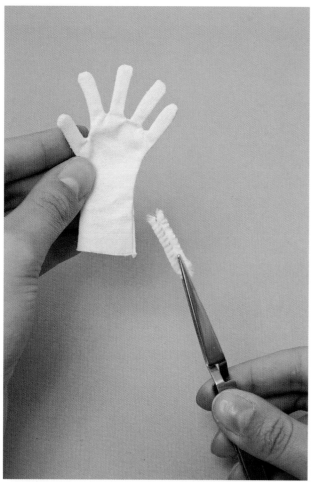

Use tweezers or hemostat to guide pipe cleaner into each finger.

4. Grab a very small bit of stuffing with the reverse-action tweezers and guide it to the opening of the finger in the palm of the hand. Use the solid rod from the set of turning tubes to push the stuffing all the way to the tip of the finger. Take another small bit of stuffing and guide it to the opening of the finger on the back side of the hand, and then use the solid rod to push the stuffing to the fingertip. Continue stuffing the finger by alternating back and forth on both sides of the pipe cleaner, gently packing the stuffing each time so the finger is firm.

When you are finished, the pipe cleaner will be in the center of the finger with stuffing on both sides. This will create a nicely rounded finger. If you stuff only on one side of the

pipe cleaner, the finger will be flat on one side. Stuff all 5 fingers this way before stuffing the palm of the hand. Resist the urge to bend the fingers until the entire hand and arm are stuffed.

STUFFING THE HANDS AND ARMS

When all the fingers are wired and stuffed, the ends of the pipe cleaners will be sticking out into the palm of the hand.

1. In much the same way that you encircled the pipe cleaners with stuffing in the fingers, stuff the hand.

Make sure the opening of each finger has enough stuffing in it, so it is not flat. Use tweezers to guide stuffing on the palm side of the hand and on the back side of the hand, so the pipe cleaners are sandwiched in the middle. Once you stuff past the pipe cleaners, you can add larger bits of stuffing and use your stuffing tool of choice.

2. Stuff the rest of the arm firmly. The wrists tend to get a wrinkle and bend in them if they are not stuffed firmly enough. Once the arm is stuffed, it is very difficult to fix this problem, so pay attention to this area as you stuff.

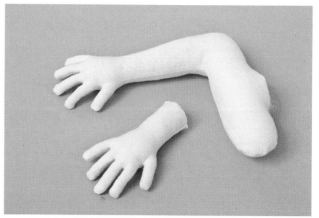

Stuff hand and arm firmly.

I often wait until the doll is complete before bending the fingers. Once I've decided whether it will be holding anything and its position, I wrap the fingers around a pencil for a nice curve. Wire can easily get a kink in it, so try not to manipulate them too much.

Refer to the specific project instructions to attach the arms and hands.

Constructing the Head

From left to right: Abby, Estelle, and Jilly

Each doll in this book has a different-shaped head, but the heads are all made the same way.

1. Notice that the head pieces have a sewing line on one side and a cutting line on the other side. Sew the 2 seams on the head back around the stuffing hole. Then sew the center seam of the head front.

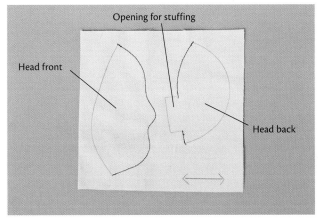

Opening for stuffing

Head front

Head back

Example is sewn with red thread for clarity.

2. Cut out each piece ⅛" outside the sewing lines.

3. On the cutting lines that you did not sew, cut on the pencil lines.

4. Open the head front and back and pin them with right sides together.

The opening for turning and stuffing is also where the neck connects to the head, so make sure the head front (the side with the nose) is not upside down.

5. Match the center seams at the top of the head and pin together.

6. Then, match the center seams at the chin and pin together.

7. Once the seams are matched up, pin together both sides of the head.

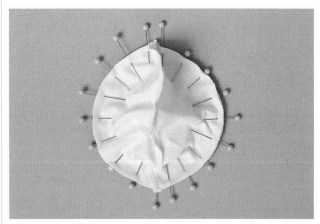

Use many pins.

Use many pins, as shown in the photo, so that you don't ease the fabric or end up with puckers.

NOTE

Often when we sew, we ease the fabric to make it fit when one side has more slack in it than the other. This means pulling or stretching one side of the fabric to make it fit. Never ease the fabric on any of the body pieces, as this may twist or distort the finished piece. Take the time to pin the fabric, and the result will be smooth seams.

8. Sew around the head with a ⅛" seam allowance, taking out the pins as you sew. Turn the head right side out.

9. Stuff the head loosely at first. Use a dowel or pencil to push stuffing into the nose. Then stuff around the side seam all the way around the head. Push ample stuffing into the chin, forehead, and cheeks. Leave an open space at the stuffing hole for the neck to be inserted later.

Sculpting the Head

The head should be sculpted and the face painted before it is attached to the body. I also prefer dressing the doll before attaching the head. It is much easier to dress the body without the head in the way.

Sculpted heads can be very detailed, right down to bags under the eyes or dimples in the cheeks. I suggest that you start simply with the nose and mouth. With each head you make, you can add more detail.

Kona Cotton has a minimal amount of stretch, but it is more than enough to bring shape to the face.

MARKING THE SCULPTING STITCHES

1. Use straight pins to mark the sculpting stitches. Move the pins around until you are happy with the placement. Pins 2 and 4 are indentations for the nostril openings; 1 and 5 will form the left nostril; 3 and 6 will form the right nostril; 9 and 10 are the corners of the mouth; and 7, 8, and 11 are couching stitches to hold the sculpting thread in place. Use the center seam of the head as a guide so the pins on the right side of the face are spaced the same as those on the left side of the face. You want the nose to be straight and each side to be the same size.

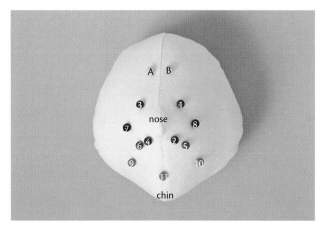

Use straight pins to mark sculpting stitches.

2. Use a disappearing fabric marker or water-soluble marker to draw the guides on the face. The marks will be erased later when the face is wet while painting.

Draw a guideline on each side of the nose that starts at the bridge of the nose at A and B and ends at pins 1 and 3. The line should angle out slightly as it comes down to the nostril. Pull the pins out one at a time and use the marker to make dots in their place.

Wiggle the pin as you pull it out, and it will leave a hole in the fabric to mark.

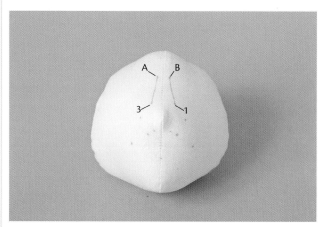

Draw guidelines.

3. Use a strong quilting thread and a 4″ to 7″ needle for sculpting. The needle needs to be long enough to reach from the back of the head to all the marks on the face. If the needle is too short, you will find yourself frustrated as you poke around trying to hit the right spot.

Thread the needle with a 30″ to 40″ length of thread and knot the end.

You don't need to try to sculpt the entire face with one length of thread. You can begin a new length of thread as needed.

The center seam at the back of the head will be the starting and stopping point for the thread. The seam will give you a place to tie off the thread, and the knots will be hidden later by the hair. Read through the entire sculpting process before you begin. Then take it one step at a time. After you have worked through the whole process, you will have a better understanding of it and it will actually become fun.

SCULPTING THE BRIDGE OF THE NOSE

1. Begin by going in at the seam on the back of the head and coming out at the bridge of the nose at A.

As you take a sculpting stitch, push in on that area with your finger so the tension of the thread doesn't make a hole in the fabric.

2. Beginning at the top of the nose, take small stitches, one at a time, along the guidelines, alternating from one side of the nose to the other. Continue stitching on alternating sides until you reach the top of the nostrils at pins 1 and 3. Keep the stitches on each side of the nose the same distance from the center seam in the face.

3. When you reach the top of the nostrils at pins 1 and 3, take the thread to the back of the head and knot to hold the tension. Continue with the same thread or start a new thread if needed.

Sculpt bridge of nose.

NOTE

Sewing the bridge of the nose is optional. Kitty (page 47) does not have this sculpting step.

SCULPTING THE NOSTRILS

1. Begin by going in at the seam on the back of the head and coming out at pin 1 (top of the left nostril).

2. Take a small stitch, going back in at 1, and come out at 2 (left nostril). Take a small stitch, going back in at 2, and come out at 3 (top of the right nostril). With your index finger and thumb, pinch together stitches 1 and 2 and pull the slack out of the thread.

3. Take a small stitch to go back in at 3 and come out at 4 (right nostril). Take a small stitch and go back in at 4 and come out at 1. Use your index finger and thumb to pinch together stitches 3 and 4 and pull the slack out of the thread.

Pull slack out of thread to sculpt nostrils.

4. Stick pins in the marks at 7 and 8. The pins will hold the thread in place until you add the couching stitch.

5. From 1, take the thread around the pin at 8, and go in at 5, and come out at 3.

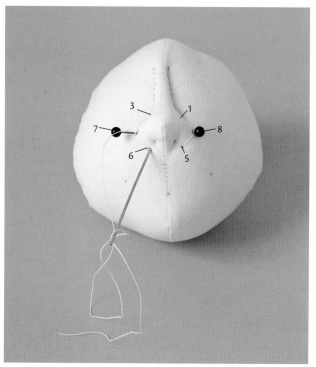

Form nostril.

Again using your fingers, pinch together at 1 and 5 and pull the slack out of the thread. The pin at 8 will hold the thread to make a half circle and form the left nostril.

6. Repeat the same steps to make the right nostril. Go from 3, around pin 7, and in at 6 and come out at the seam on the back of the head. Pull the slack out of the thread forming the right nostril and tie off the thread, keeping the tension. Knotting the thread will hold the tension in the sculpting stitches. You can continue if you have enough thread, or you can begin a new length of thread.

7. Start from the seam on the back of the head and come out at pin 8 on one side of the nostril thread, take a tiny stitch, going back in on the opposite side of the thread, and come out at pin 7. Pull just enough tension to hold the nostril thread in place without creating a big dimple.

8. Make a couching stitch (page 9) to hold the thread in place at pins 7 and 8.

9. After the couching stitch at pin 7, come out at the back of the head. Even though you may have enough thread to continue, tie off after completing the couching stitches so you can control the amount of tension. You have just completed a basic nose.

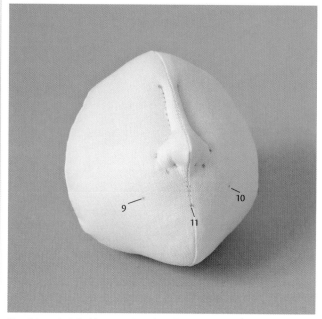

Couching stitch holds nose wing thread in place. Marks 9, 10, and 11 are used for sculpting the mouth.

SCULPTING THE MOUTH

Pins 9 and 10 are the corners of the mouth, and pin 11 marks the couching stitch. The space between 9 and 10 will be the width of the lips. The shape of the lips is an individual choice and certainly one that can give a specific look or attitude to your doll.

1. Start at the seam on the back of the head and come out at 9, take a tiny stitch, going back in at 9, and come out at the back of the head. Push the stitch in with your finger and pull the slack out of the thread. Take a stitch on the back center seam and knot it to hold the tension.

2. From the back of the head, come out at 10. Take a tiny stitch and go back in at 10 and come out at the back of the head. Push the stitch in with your finger and pull the slack out of the thread, and then tie off to hold the tension.

3. Put a pin back in at 11 to help make a couching stitch. From the back of the head, come out at 9, go around the pin at 11 and in at 10, and come out the back of the head. Use your fingers to push in at 9 and 10 and pull the slack out of the thread. Tie off at the back of the head to hold the tension.

Couching stitches hold mouth thread in place.

4. Start at the back of the head, come out at pin 11, and make a couching stitch to hold the thread in place, and then tie off at the back of the head. This line will represent the separation between the upper and lower lips.

To make a wider mouth, you can take several smaller stitches instead of one large stitch. Jilly (page 60) and Mallory (page 69) have 4 stitches to create a wide smile.

This is a simple sculpted face. You can certainly go on from there and experiment. Pulling the thread tension in a different direction will give another look. For example, instead of pulling the corners of the mouth at 9 and 10 toward the back of the head, you could go from 9 to 10 and pull the corners of the mouth toward each other. You can add stitches at the corners of the eyes. Once you are comfortable sculpting a face, have some fun and experiment.

Look at the template for the head front. Notice the shape of the forehead, nose, and chin. You can change the shape of one or all of these, and your doll will have a different face. Changing the center seam on the head front will not change the side seams where the head front attaches to the head back. Keeping the side seam unchanged, you could round the chin more or make it more pronounced. Look at the people around you—their faces come in so many shapes.

As I said earlier, the head does not require much fabric, so if you really don't like it, you can pull the stuffing out and reuse it. If the head turns out nicely but doesn't look like it belongs on the doll's body, set the head aside for another doll and try again.

PAINTING THE FACE

All the dolls in this book have faces that are drawn with watercolor pencils and blended with paintbrushes. The pencils give the face a soft look, and they are easy to blend on wet fabric. There are several types and brands of colored pencils on the market. Be sure that you choose *watercolor* pencils. You will also need 2 stiff, blunt paintbrushes—a larger one for wetting the fabric and blending the cheek color, and a smaller one for blending the colors of the eyes and lips.

You may want to save a practice head for testing the pencil colors. I find that some of the colors blend more easily than others. Some colors tend to bleed on the damp fabric, while others don't bleed at all. The white, brown, yellow, and green don't bleed, but the blue, red, and black seem to bleed more readily. You will get a feel for the colors once you work with them.

The head fabric should be damp but not wet when you are coloring. If the colors are bleeding, you know the fabric is too wet. If the colors aren't blending well, you know that the fabric is too dry. It doesn't take long for the fabric to dry, so if the head is too wet just wait a few minutes before coloring. Find that happy medium so the fabric is just *damp.* Use a small cup or bowl for water and replace with clean water as needed. Make sure you clean your brush between colors so your doll won't end up with blue cheeks.

Eyes

The following instructions are for eyes with fabric eyelids. See the note on page 26 if you prefer the eyes to have drawn eyelids.

1. Use the larger paintbrush to wet the entire face, just past the side seams that connect the head front to the head back. If the fabric shows a water mark after it is dry, it will be hidden beyond the hairline.

2. Using the lightest brown watercolor pencil you have (such as terra-cotta), trace the eye template onto the face or draw your own eyes. Use a very light touch to draw the outline. If the line is very light, you will be able to erase a mistake with a wet paintbrush in a scrubbing motion.

3. Draw a circle in each eye for the iris. You can put the iris in the center of the eye or looking off to one side. Draw the iris as a whole circle. The eyelid will cover the top of the iris.

4. Use a white watercolor pencil to color the white part of the eye.

Outline eye, draw circle for iris, and color white of eye.

5. Decide on the eye color and choose a light, a medium, and a dark in that color. Then choose a yellow for a highlight. Outline the iris with the darkest color. Color ⅙ of the iris with the yellow, ⅙ with the light, and ⅔ with the medium pencils, as shown below.

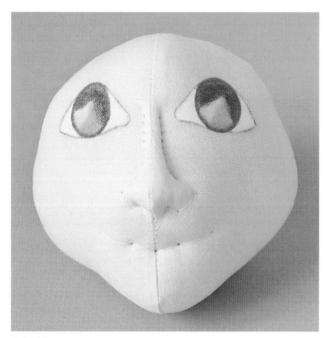

Color iris.

6. Use a small paintbrush to blend the colors of the iris together. You can add more light or dark color and blend again if you need to. If the fabric is dry and doesn't blend easily, you can wet the brush. Be careful not to add too much water, as it may cause the color on the eyes to bleed. Color both eyes at the same time so you can keep the colors somewhat even.

7. Use black to draw a circle for the pupil and color it in.

8. Choose a darker brown than you originally sketched the outline of the eye with and darken the outline. Add just a hint of red for the tear duct.

9. A tiny white dot at the edge of the pupil, on the side of the iris with the lighter highlight, will bring the eye to life. You can dip the tip of the white pencil into water to make the dot or use white acrylic paint applied with a toothpick.

10. Make short strokes with a very sharp pencil to add eyelashes to the bottom of the eye.

11. Use short, quick pencil strokes to draw the eyebrows. Try using 2 colors of brown in the eyebrow.

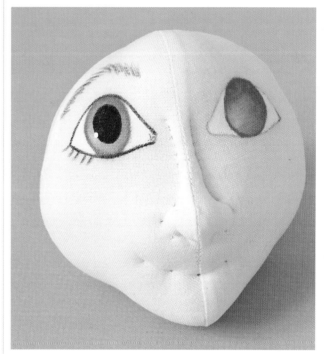

The eyelid will be added (pages 28–29) after the rest of the face is colored.

NOTE

Option: You can choose to add drawn eyelids instead of fabric ones. The drawn eyelid will cover the top of the iris, so do not draw the iris as a complete circle. Look in the mirror at your own eye. You can see almost every bit of the bottom of the iris, but the top edge of the iris is covered by the eyelid. Use a light to medium brown (depending on how dark the fabric is) to draw the crease in the eyelid. Use the side of the pencil to rub some color on the eyelid and then blend it with the paintbrush to shade the lid. Use short, quick pencil strokes on the upper and lower lids for lashes.

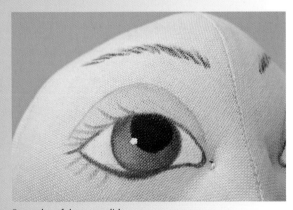

Examples of drawn eyelids

Cheeks

If the fabric has dried, use a clean paintbrush to rewet the cheeks and mouth area. If it is too wet, wait a few minutes before you begin. Choose a red, pink, or peach for a blush on the cheeks. A true red may be a little harsh on the cheeks unless you are making a rag doll and you want an exaggerated look.

You may want to try a few colors on a practice head or a scrap piece of fabric before using them on the face. Wet the scrap fabric and rub some color on with the side of the pencil. Use the paintbrush to blend the color. You may want to write the names of the colors and save the scrap to use as a guide for future dolls. Along with reds and pinks, try orange and peach colors; they also look nice on the cheeks. Try adding a little blush to the forehead and chin. A light brown blended on the sides of the nose will help give depth. It's almost like putting on your own makeup. Don't be afraid to experiment.

1. Rub the side of the pencil on the cheeks with a light hand. It's always easier to add more color than to try to blend some away. Apply the blush along the cheekbone area or in more of a circle, depending on the look you want.

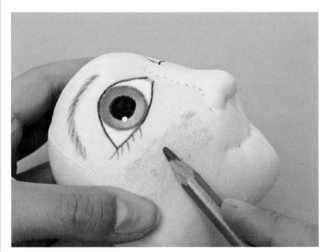

Color with side, not tip, of pencil.

2. Blend the color with a large paintbrush. When the fabric dries, the color will be slightly lighter.

Lips

If you use a peach color as a blush, choose peaches for the lips also. If your doll is a boy, choose a more natural lip color. Make sure to color the thread (the separation between the lips). Just like noses, lips come in many shapes. The lips can change the look and attitude of the face. Choose a light-, a medium-, and a dark-colored watercolor pencil for the lips.

1. Draw the outline of the lips with a pale color and a very light hand to get the shape you want.

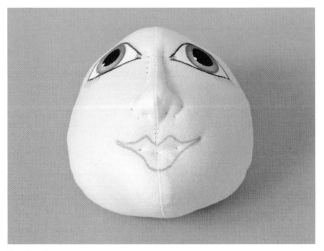

Outline lips.

2. Fill in with the medium pencil, and then use the light and dark pencils to shade.

3. Outline the lips with the dark pencil. Blend the colors with a small paintbrush.

Shade lips with light and dark pencils.

Eyelids and Eyelashes

The eyelids are made from the body fabric. You can leave the fabric as is or add color with the watercolor pencils. If you want to add color, shade the eyelids with a light brown or completely color them as if they have eye shadow. Wet the fabric, color, and then blend with a paintbrush. You could also add a black line for eyeliner. To speed up the process, dry the fabric with a hair dryer or iron.

An alternative to coloring fabric is to use fabric that is already the color you want. For a subtle look, use a fabric that is a shade darker than the fabric you used for the doll body. For a more severe look, choose a brightly colored fabric for the eyelid.

1. Use iron-on fusible web sandwiched between 2 squares of eyelid fabric 2" × 2". With the iron, fuse the 2 fabrics together.

2. Use a mechanical pencil to lightly trace the eyelid templates or draw your own lids. The lid is just slightly wider than the eye.

3. Carefully cut out the eyelids. The fusible web will help the eyelids hold their shape and keep the edges from fraying. If you choose to have black eyeliner, draw the line on the fabric before you cut out the eyelid. You will get a much nicer line than if you try to draw on the edge after you cut out the eyelid.

Cut out eyelids in fused fabric.

There are many sources for eyelashes. I prefer to use individual eyelash bunches. I use the type that you might buy for yourself at the drug or grocery store. They are inexpensive and easy to find. Some of the lashes made for dolls are plastic looking, which I don't find very appealing, and the eyelash strips never seem to be the right size. You can cut the strips, but what is left never seems to be enough for the other lid and is just wasted. The eyelash bunches allow you to use as many or as few as you like. Depending on the size of the doll, one box is enough for 3 or 4 faces.

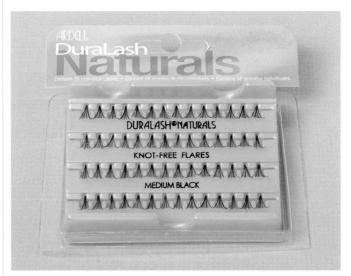
Lashes come in short, medium, and long.

4. Use white craft glue that dries clear to attach the lashes. Grasp the eyelid at the top with the reverse-action tweezers. Lay the tweezers on the table with the back side of the lid facing up.

5. Put a dab of glue on a scrap of paper. Pick up an eyelash bunch with regular tweezers and dip the end in glue. Attach the bunches along the bottom edge of the backside of the lid. Let the glue dry completely before gluing the lid to the face.

Apply bunches to back side of lid.

6. The eyelid is a little larger than the eye to allow the lid to be slightly cupped over the eye. Run a thin line of glue along the inside of the top of the lid with a toothpick (not the edge with the lashes). Place the lid over the eye, pressing the glued edge above the eye. There should be a little space between the eye and the lashes, but not so much that you can see all the way under the lid. The small amount of glue will adhere quickly and you won't be able to make adjustments, so make sure you put the lid where you want it the first time.

Lid is cupped slightly, so lashes are not touching eye.

Attaching the Head

Now that the head is complete, you can attach it to the completed body; however, it is much easier to finish dressing the body before attaching the head, and there is less chance of messing up the eyelashes. The head may look a bit awkward at this point, but as soon as you give your doll some hair, it will all come together. Push the neck into the stuffing hole of the head. If you can't get the neck far enough into the head to be secure, remove a little bit of stuffing. Pin the head to the neck to hold it in place as you sew. Use the ladder stitch (page 9) to attach the head to the neck. The top of the neck is far enough up at the back of the head that the seam will be hidden by the hair.

Creating a Hairstyle

Adding the right hairstyle will bring a lot of personality to your doll. First, you need to choose the material. The theme of the doll or a specific look that you have in mind will help you choose the material to use for the hair. I've tried to use a variety of materials on the dolls throughout this book to help inspire you.

The only time I use glue is for the eyelashes and the construction of some props. While you could use glue to attach the hair, I don't recommend it. When the glue hardens, the fabric also becomes stiff.

Examples of synthetic hair

HAIR MATERIALS

Synthetic doll hair comes in large and small curls, straight, braids, and wigs. It is available in a range of blondes, brunettes, blacks, and reds. Most craft stores carry a small selection. If you can't find what you're looking for, try searching online for a wide selection. Synthetic doll hair is sewn onto the head. You may find that after the hair has had a few days to relax, you will need to snip off a few strands that have stretched a bit too long. You can also use hair spray to help hold the hair in place. Cover the face and clothes with scraps of paper, using pins to hold the paper in place, and then spray the hair. Several dolls in this book have synthetic hair. Phyllis (page 45) has small curls, Lorna (page 58) has large curls, Maisie (page 59) has crimped hair, and Kitty (page 47) has straight hair.

Yarn is available in many colors and textures, and makes wonderful hair. Look beyond the smooth yarns to the bumpy, fuzzy, and stringy skeins. Some are made with multiple textures in the same strand as well as multiple colors. You could also combine 2 or more yarns to create your own look. If you're looking for something a little more subtle, choose a textured yarn in brown, black, or yellow. Abby (page 32), Iris (page 46), Cecelia (page 44), Mallory (page 69), and Jilly (page 60) all have yarn hair.

Examples of wool yarn and roving

Wool or wool blended with alpaca, llama, or goat hair can be used for hair. It is attached to the head with felting needles. It is a fun and easy way to attach hair. It will also give you options for making parts in the hair without using thread. You can find loosely twisted wool yarns or chunky yarns. You could also use roving. Roving has been cleaned and combed and is ready to spin into yarn. You can find it at yarn shops or online, sold by the ounce. If you live in a farming area, you might be able to find it locally. Estelle (page 49) has hair that is made from a loosely twisted yarn that is a blend of wool and alpaca. The yarn was untwisted and felted to the head. Wool roving was used for the hair, mustache, and eyebrows

Examples of yarn

on Chef Caesar Selid (page 48). A metal comb can be used to comb the wool and smooth out the fibers.

Felting needles are very sharp, with tiny barbs at the end. The wool is laid on the doll head, and in a quick motion the needle is poked through the wool and into the doll head. The barbs on the needle grab the wool, pulling the fibers into the head and tangling them with the stuffing. Felting is not new but seems to be growing in popularity.

Beyond the obvious yarns and synthetic doll hair, there are still more options. Look on the shelf of trims at your favorite fabric store. Fringe can be sewed to the head in a spiral pattern. Trims with sequins and beads are also interesting. A couple of the rag dolls in this book have shoelace yarn for hair. It comes in a skein like yarn and looks like an unending shoelace. It will give the same effect as sewing strips of fabric to the head but without all the fraying threads. Ribbon yarn gives the same effect. It is not yarn but ribbon wrapped on a spool like twine.

Shoelace ribbon yarn

I hope the techniques in this chapter, along with the individual projects in this book, will lead you to a fun and successful doll-making experience as you create your own unique fabric friends.

CHAPTER TWO

ABBY
16" Standing Doll

Materials

- ½ yard Kona Cotton for body
- ¼ yard fabric for blouse
- ⅜ yard fabric for jacket and hat
- ¼ yard fabric for trim on jacket and hat
- ¼ yard fabric for skirt
- ¼ yard fabric for underwear
- 7" × 20" piece of imitation leather or vinyl for shoes and purse
- 1 white knee-high (or little girl's tights) for socks
- 18" of ¼"-wide trim for blouse neckline and sleeves (You can add or omit trims as desired.)
- 18" of ¼"- or ½"-wide trim for legs of undergarment
- 8" of 1"-wide (or wider) lace trim for bra
- 5 tiny buttons for blouse (In place of the tiny buttons you could also use beads or small charms. Anything that is small enough to be in proportion would work.)
- 4 tiny buttons for jacket
- 6 tiny buttons for shoes
- 1 tiny button for purse
- Loopy yarn for hair (approximately ¼ skein)
- 2 white pipe cleaners for fingers
- Polyester fiberfill
- Coordinating thread for sewing
- Strong quilting thread to sculpt face in color to match face
- Artist-quality watercolor pencils for painting face
- 1 package false eyelashes (You could omit the lashes and draw them instead [page 26].)
- 3" × 3" piece of fusible web for eyelids

Embellishments

The list of items for embellishing shows what was used for the project doll. If you choose a different theme you could come up with your own list of items that are made or purchased ready-made.

- 3½" chain for bracelet
- Tiny charms to hang off bracelet
- ¼"-wide jump rings for finger rings
- 3 wooden thread spools ½" tall
- Seed beads for necklace
- 26" length of ⅛"-wide ribbon (or string) for shopping bag handles and to tie fabric in shopping bag
- 8½" × 11" sheet of cardstock for shopping bags
- Scraps of fabric and ribbon for items in shopping bags

TEMPLATES REQUIRED

Find the template patterns beginning on page 96. Make templates following the instructions on page 13.

Head Front A, Head Back A, Body A, Leg A, Hand A, Arm A, Arm B, Breast, Blouse Front A, Blouse Back A, Shorts Center Front, Shorts Back, Shorts Side Front, Jacket Front, Jacket Back, Jacket Sleeve, Jacket Edging, Hat Top, Shoe Sole A, Shoe Top A, Shoe Strap C, Purse, Purse Strap, Shopping Bag, Eye, Eyelid

Constructing the Body

Before you begin, review Chapter 1, The Cloth Doll: Basic Body Construction (pages 10–31). As you are sewing, you can refer back to Chapter 1 any time you feel you need additional direction. Read through all the project instructions before you begin.

Tracing, Sewing, and Cutting

1. Find the direction of stretch on the body fabric and draw an arrow at the edge of the fabric in the direction of the stretch to use as a guide (page 14).

2. Lay out the templates on 2 layers of fabric, right sides together, matching the arrow on each template to the arrow you marked on the fabric, for Head Front A, Head Back A, Body A, Arm A, Arm B, Hand A, Leg A, and Breast.

3. Use a mechanical pencil to neatly trace around each template. Trace the leg twice and the hand twice. Make your pencil lines just dark enough to see. If the lines are too dark, they may show through light-colored fabric. On each piece, identify the dashed sewing lines, the solid cutting lines, and the openings for turning and stuffing. Shorten the stitch length on your machine and use the smallest stitch when sewing around the fingers (page 16). Take your time and sew directly on the pencil lines.

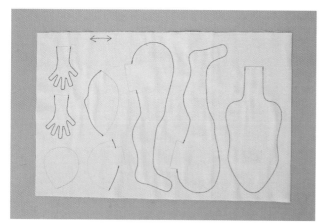

Sew with thread to match fabric. Sample has been sewn with red thread to make stitching easier to see.

4. Cut out each piece with a ⅛″ seam allowance. On the cutting lines that you did not sew, cut out directly on the pencil lines.

Stuffing the Body

1. Use turning tubes to turn the fingers right side out (page 17).

2. Wire the fingers (pages 17–18), and stuff the hands.

3. Finish sewing, stuffing, and painting the head (pages 19–29).

4. Turn the body right side out. Stuff the doll body through the opening in the neck. Make sure there is ample stuffing in the neck so it doesn't wrinkle. The neck may seem long, but there needs to be enough to push up into the head to make it secure. Whipstitch the neck closed. This seam will be hidden when the head is attached.

5. Turn both legs right side out. Stuff each leg firmly from the toes up to the middle of the thigh. Stuff the rest of the thigh area so it is soft. The top of the thigh will be wrapped around the side of the body, so it needs to be soft enough to manipulate.

Attaching the Legs

1. Pin the legs to the body, wrapping the thighs around the hips. The hips need to be in line so that one leg is not longer than the other and the doll stands straight.

2. Starting at the top of the hip, use a ladder stitch (page 9) to sew around the inside of the leg and back up to the hip.

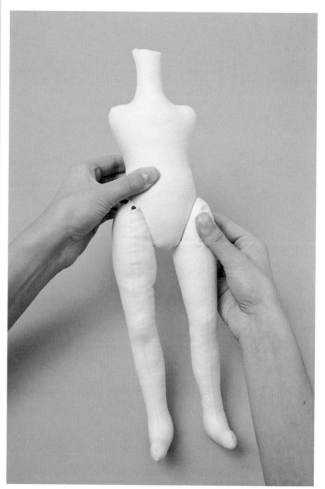

Pin and stitch thigh to hip.

Making the Arms

1. The arms are made from the blouse fabric and templates Arm A and Arm B. This doll has 2 differently shaped arms to pose properly. Find the direction of stretch on the body fabric. Draw an arrow at the edge of the fabric in the direction of the stretch to use as a guide.

2. Lay out the arm templates on 2 layers of fabric, right sides together, matching the arrow on each template to the arrow you marked on the fabric. Use a mechanical pencil to neatly trace around each template. Pin the fabric together.

3. Identify the dashed sewing lines and the solid cutting lines. Sew around the arm.

4. Cut out each arm with a ⅛″ seam allowance. Turn the arms right side out and stuff firmly.

5. Fold under the raw edges of fabric ½″ at the wrist on each arm and hand. Pin the hands to the arms, matching up the seams. Make sure the thumbs are pointing in the proper direction, depending on how you will pose your doll. Ladder stitch the hands to the arms. Add a little more stuffing before closing the ladder stitch to make sure the wrists are firm.

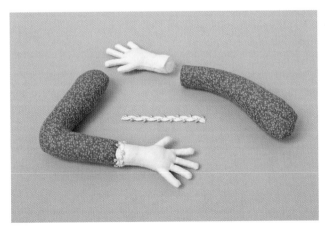

Trim will cover wrist seam.

6. Cut a 2½″ length of trim for each wrist. Wrap the trim around the wrist so that it covers the seam where the arm and hand join. Choose a thread color to match the trim so the stitches are not seen. Stitch the trim on with tiny stitches around the wrist.

7. Set the arms aside for now. The blouse will be made and put on the doll before the arms are attached.

Making the Breasts and Bra

1. Cut 2 breast pieces from the body fabric, making certain that one breast is the mirror image of the other. Sew 3 darts in each one, as shown on the template pattern.

2. Place each breast in place with the pointed edge on top near the shoulder and the fuller, rounded edge toward the middle of the chest. Pin each breast to the chest, folding the raw edge under ¼″.

3. Ladder stitch the breast to the chest. Begin sewing on the side of the body and sew around the breast. Stop about ¾″ from where you started, but don't end the thread. Stuff the breast firmly and then continue sewing to close the stuffing hole. Sew and stuff the other breast the same way.

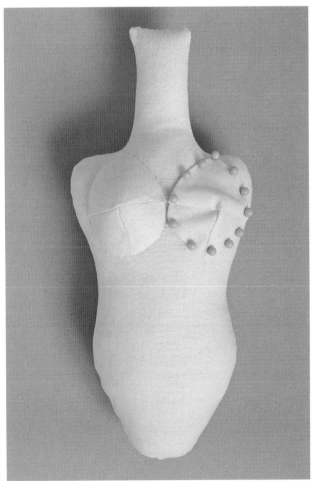

Pin and then stitch breast to chest.

4. For the bra, cut 2 pieces of lace trim 3" long. The width of the lace can be 1" or wider. Just the edge of the trim will show from the neckline of the blouse, so it is not important to cover the entire breast area.

5. Pin the lace to the bust area. Use a matching thread color to sew the lace to the body. You may find that a curved needle will work better than a straight needle here.

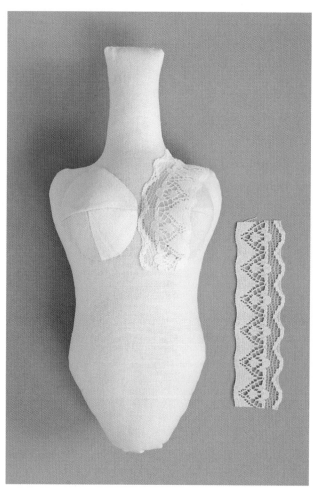

Place lace around curve of breast, so it will lie flat.

Dressing the Doll

All the clothes have ¼" seam allowances included in the template patterns unless otherwise stated. It is best to have an iron handy and press open the seams of each garment as you sew.

Underwear

1. For the underwear, use the Shorts Center Front, Shorts Side Front, and Shorts Back templates. Lay out 2 layers of fabric, with right sides together. Pin the templates to the fabric, and then trace and cut out.

2. With right sides together, sew the 2 back pieces together at the center back seam, starting at the crotch and stopping 1½" before the waist.

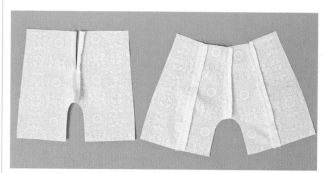

Center back seam is sewn halfway to allow underwear to be put on doll.

3. With right sides together, sew the 2 center front pieces together at the center front seam.

4. With right sides together, sew 1 side front piece to each side of the shorts center front.

5. With right sides together, pin the front to the back at the crotch and sew around the crotch seam.

6. Sew darts in the waist that are about 1" long. Darts should be sewn in the center of each back piece and in the center of each side front piece. Try the underwear on the doll and adjust the darts if needed, so the waist fits snugly.

7. With the underwear on the doll body, fold under the bottom edge of the shorts leg so that it is just above the knee. Pin.

8. With the side seam of the shorts still open, sew a hem across the shorts legs. Add a ¼"- to ½"-wide piece of trim to each leg. Depending on the trim that you choose, you could sew the trim at the bottom edge of the shorts leg or ½" up from the bottom edge.

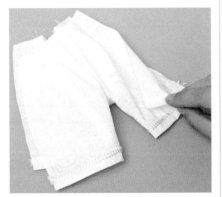

Sew hem and trim on each leg before sewing side seams.

> **NOTE**
> Sew the hem and any trims on the shorts and sleeves before sewing the side seams or they may be too small to fit under the presser foot of the sewing machine.

9. With right sides together, matching up the bottom edges of the shorts legs, sew the side seams of the shorts.

10. Turn the underwear right side out and put it on the doll body.

11. Fold under the raw edge of the shorts opening at the back. Ladder stitch the shorts closed so the waist fits snugly. Take a few stitches around the waist, sewing the shorts to the body so they stay in place. The raw edge at the top of the shorts will be hidden by the skirt.

Waist fits snugly on body.

Skirt

1. There is no template for the skirt. The skirt is made from a 7″ × 16″ rectangle. Use a ruler and a pencil to draw the rectangle on the wrong side of the fabric and then cut it out. You could also use an acrylic quilting ruler and a rotary cutter.

Bottom edge of skirt is hemmed and top edge is gathered.

2. Sew the 2 short (7″) sides of the 7″ × 16″ rectangle together, making a tube.

3. Sew a ¼" hem in one end of the tube. This will be the bottom edge of the skirt.

4. Sew a gathering stitch (see page 9) on the other side of the tube, about ¼" from the edge of the fabric. This will be the waist of the skirt.

5. Put the skirt on the doll. Pull the gathering stitch until the skirt fits snugly around the waist. Line up the seam in the skirt at the center back of the doll. Evenly space the gathers around the waist and pin the skirt to the body.

6. Choose a thread that matches the skirt and sew the waist of the skirt to the doll body. The blouse will cover the raw edge at the top of the skirt.

Blouse

1. Fold the blouse fabric with right sides together. Use the templates for Blouse Front A and Blouse Back A. Note that Blouse Back A should be cut on the fold. Pin the templates to the fabric, and then trace and cut out.

2. With right sides together, pin the blouse fronts to the blouse back at the shoulders/sides. Sew the sides and the shoulders in a single seam.

3. Turn right side out and try the blouse on the doll. Turn under the hem of the blouse so that it covers the top edge of the skirt. Pin. Take the blouse off the doll and sew the hem in the bottom edge of the blouse.

4. Using the same trim that you put on the wrists, sew trim around the neckline of the blouse.

There are no armholes on blouse.

5. Put the blouse on the doll. Fold under the raw edges at the front of the blouse. Sew 5 tiny buttons or beads to one side of the blouse. Use a ladder stitch to close the front opening of the blouse.

Attaching the Arms

1. Pin the arms to the body at the shoulders.

2. Choose a thread color that matches the blouse and sew the arms to the body using the ladder stitch.

Position arms to accommodate props they will be holding.

Jacket

1. Fold the jacket fabric with right sides together. Use the templates Jacket Front, Jacket Back, and Jacket Sleeve. Jacket Back and Jacket Sleeve should be placed on the fold. Pin the templates to the fabric, and then trace and cut out.

2. For the jacket trim, fold a single layer of fabric with right sides together. Pin the Jacket Edging template to the fabric on the fold and cut out.

3. There are no templates for the trim at the bottom edge of the jacket and the sleeves. For the sleeve trim, cut 2 rectangles 1½" × 6". For the trim at the bottom edge of the jacket, cut 1 rectangle 1½" × 12".

4. Sew the jacket back to the jacket fronts at the shoulders.

5. Pin the jacket edging to the jacket front opening with right sides together. Sew in place and remove the pins. Turn right side out and iron the trim so that ¼″ of the trim shows on the outside of the jacket.

6. With right sides together, pin the sleeve trim to the bottom edge of the sleeve and sew in place. Iron each sleeve so that ¼″ of the trim shows on the outside of the sleeve. Sew across the sleeve, creating a hem.

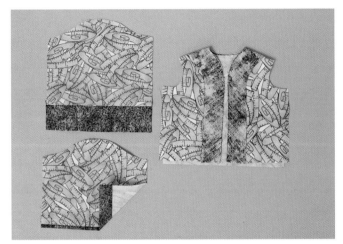

Trim fabric is sewn to sleeve edge and jacket opening and is then hemmed.

7. With right sides together, pin each sleeve to the armhole of the jacket and sew around the armhole.

8. Sew the underside of the sleeve and the jacket side in a single seam.

9. With right sides together, pin the 1½″ × 12″ trim to the bottom edge of the jacket. Sew in place and remove the pins. Iron the bottom edge so that ¼″ of the trim shows on the outside of the jacket. You can sew around the bottom edge of the jacket, up the front, and around the collar all in a single seam.

Completed jacket, shown inside out

10. Sew 4 tiny buttons or beads to one side of the jacket front. Put the jacket on the doll.

Hat

1. Lay out 1 layer of the jacket fabric. Pin the Hat Top template to the fabric, and then trace and cut out.

2. The rim of the hat does not have a template. Use the same fabric that was used for the trim on the jacket and cut a 2″ × 17″ rectangle.

3. With right sides together, fold the rim in half lengthwise. Sew the hat rim at each short end on an angle and down the long edge, leaving a hole in the middle of the long edge to turn right side out.

Leave open.

Sew leaving opening in center.

4. Turn the rim right side out. (You can use the finger turning tubes.) Press.

5. Tie a knot in the ends of the rim so it makes a loop that is about 10″ around.

6. Sew a gathering stitch around the edge of the hat circle. Pull the thread to gather the circle so it fits inside the rim.

7. Evenly space the gathers and pin the hat top inside the rim. Whipstitch the hat top to the rim on the inside. Set the hat aside.

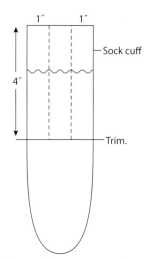

Gather hat top so it fits inside rim.

Socks and Shoes

1. Abby is wearing a short sock that is 1″ wide by 3½″ long. The socks were cut from the top of a white knee-high, using the hem that was already in the knee-high as the top of the sock. Sew 4″ down from the top of the knee-high, about 1″ in from the edge.

1″   1″

Sock cuff

4″

Trim.

Stitch a 4″ seam 1″ from each edge of knee-high sock.

2. Cut out the socks with a ⅛″ seam allowance.

3. Lay the sock so the seam is in the center, and then sew across the toe opening. Repeat for the second sock. Turn the socks right side out. Put the socks on the doll's feet so that the seam is on the bottom of the foot.

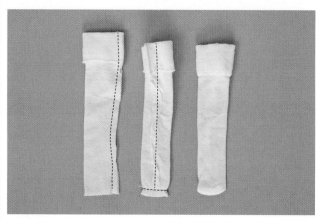

Make socks.

> # TIP
>
> Panty hose are made in the same way as the socks, except that they are longer. Gallery dolls Cecelia (page 44) and Phyllis (page 45) are wearing panty hose made this way. The top raw edge of the panty hose is rolled down to just above the knee.

4. For the shoes, use templates Shoe Sole A, Shoe Top A, and Shoe Strap C. Lay out a single layer of vinyl, wrong side up. Using a pen or fabric marker, trace each shoe template twice. The templates show a center mark on the sole at the heel and toe, and on the shoe top at the toe. Transfer these center marks to each piece. Cut out the shoes.

5. Whipstitch the shoe top to the shoe sole with wrong sides together.

If you match the thread to the vinyl, the stitches will hardly be noticeable. If you want the stitches to stand out, then choose a contrasting color of thread. With wrong sides together, line up the center marks at the toe on the shoe sole and the shoe top. You could machine stitch shoes, if you prefer.

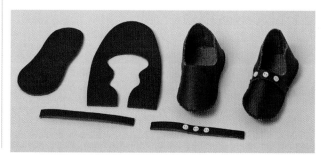

Construct shoes by hand or machine.

6. Trim off any excess shoe top at the heel so the 2 ends meet, lining up at the center mark you made on the sole at the heel. Whipstitch the 2 ends of the top together at the heel.

7. Sew 3 tiny buttons on each shoe strap.

Instead of buttons, you could attach anything that has the right proportion for the shoe—1 larger button, a charm, beads, or something that ties in with the theme of the doll. Attach the detail you choose to the center of the strap. Whipstitch each end of the strap to the seam on each side of the shoe. Put the shoes on the doll.

Finished socks and shoes

Sculpting and Painting the Face

Refer to Chapter 1, beginning on page 10, which will take you through sculpting and painting the face, adding the eyelids and lashes, and attaching the head to the body. Decide what color the doll's eyes and hair will be. We don't normally change our hair and eye color to match our outfits, but we do tend to wear colors that complement our skin tone and hair and eye color. With this in mind, you may want to choose colors that complement your doll's coloring as a whole. This also includes the colors that you choose for the lips and cheek blush. If the fabrics that you used have orange tones, for example, choose a peach color for the cheeks and lips. The size and shape of the doll's eyes, eyelids, lips, and nose will all combine to give her a unique look that is all her own.

Creating the Hairstyle

1. Abby's hair is made from a loopy yarn. Choose thread that matches the yarn color.

2. Cut 10" lengths of yarn. Pick up 5 strands at a time in the center.

3. Sew the bundles of yarn around the crown of the head. The center area of the head, where the yarn is attached, will be hidden by the hat.

Pick up strands in center and sew to head.

4. Cut 6" strands of yarn for the bangs. Pick up 5 strands at a time in the center and sew these bundles at the top of the crown, so they fall toward the forehead.

5. The thicker the yarn is, the fewer strands it will take. Add just enough so the head fabric is covered.

6. Once all the yarn is attached, give the doll a haircut to even out the ends, including the bangs.

7. Put stuffing in the hat so it will always keep its shape. Pin the hat to the head, covering all the ends where the hair is attached at the crown. Using a thread that matches the hat rim or a clear thread, stitch the hat to the head. A curved needle works best. With the needle, catch the edge of the hat rim and then go past the hair to catch the head fabric. Sew around the hat, attaching it to the head in 5 or 6 places.

Position hat so knot in rim is off to one side and then sew hat to head.

Embellishing the Doll

Abby has been shopping at her favorite fabric shop for quilting and sewing supplies. She has shopping bags full of goodies and her purse on her shoulder.

1. For the purse, use the Purse and Purse Strap templates and the same vinyl that you used for the shoes. Lay out a single layer, wrong side up. Using a pen or fabric marker, trace each template. Mark the dots as shown on each template. Cut out the purse. Match up the dots on the strap to the dots on the purse. Sew the strap to the purse with a whipstitch, using the same thread you used for the shoes. Stuff the purse with a tissue to help it keep its shape. Close the purse flap by sewing on a tiny button or bead.

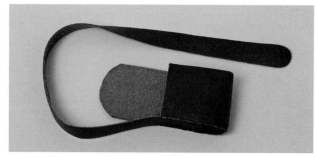

Construct purse.

Finished purse

2. Use the Shopping Bag template and trace onto cardstock. For the bag handles, cut string or ribbon into 2 pieces 6" long and tie a knot in each end. Glue the knot to the inside of the bag. Fold the bag on the fold lines and glue each flap.

Notice that the dashed lines on the bag are fold lines. You can enlarge or reduce the Shopping Bag template. I made logos and designs on my computer, printed them on cardstock, and then traced the shopping bag template on the cardstock. You could also use printed cardstock, old greeting cards, or scrapbooking paper to personalize each bag.

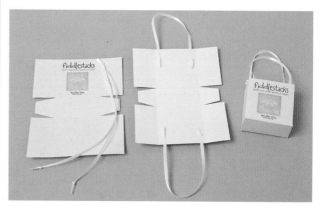

Construct shopping bag.

Arrange the contents of the shopping bags to show off the items and then glue the contents in place. Fold and stack some pieces of fabric. Cut other fabrics in 1" squares, and then stack and tie with a ⅛"-wide ribbon. Cut several coordinating fabrics into 1" strips, roll them up into a jelly roll, and tie with a ⅛"-wide ribbon. Little wooden thread spools can be found at most craft stores. Put a dab of white glue on the spool and wrap with thread. A button in the shape of scissors is a wonderful finishing touch.

Items for shopping bag shopping bag

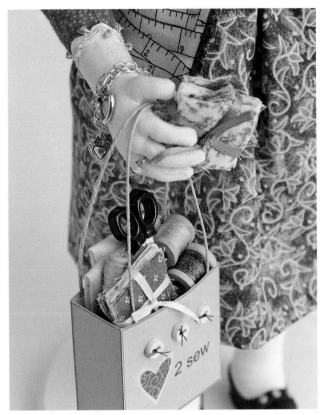

Filled shopping bag

MAKING A DOLL STAND

Your doll may stand on her own, but you will still want the security of a doll stand. You can purchase a stand or make a simple stand like the ones used in this book. Craft stores carry 5″ or 6″ unfinished pine plaques. They come in round, oval, square, and rectangular shapes with rounded edges. This type of plaque is used for the base of the doll stand.

Materials for Doll Stand

- 1 unfinished pine plaque for base
- 12″ of ½″-wide dowel
- 2″ of ⅛″-wide dowel

1. Drill a ⅛″ hole in the ½″-wide dowel, about ½″ from the end.

2. Push the 2″ dowel through the hole.

3. Drill a ½″ hole in the plaque close to one edge. Put a dab of white glue in the hole and push the unaltered end of the 12″ dowel into the hole.

4. Paint the stand and let it dry completely before using. Choose white or off-white paint so the stand doesn't distract from the doll.

5. Slide the dowel up the back of the doll's shirt to hold the doll on the stand.

3. Every girl needs jewelry. String seed beads with a needle and thread to make a 4½″ and a 5½″ necklace. Jump rings used in jewelry making are just the right size to slide on the doll's fingers. Open each jump ring and slide on a single bead to make rings for her fingers. Attach tiny charms to a 3½″ chain to make a beautiful charm bracelet. Sew a tiny safety pin to the breast of her jacket as a pin.

Make her jewelry.

Place the embellishments into position on the doll and stitch to secure.

Construct doll stand.

Cecelia

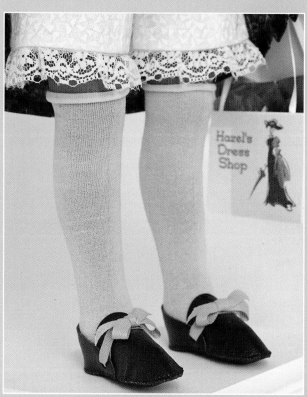

Cecelia's gloves are made using the Hand A template. Trace, sew, and cut out on white fabric. Then turn right side out and fold under the raw edge. Three-inch store-bought glasses are in perfect proportion for this 16″ doll. Pearl earrings give the illusion of ears under her hair.

Phyllis

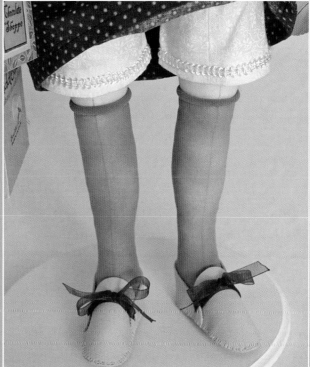

Phyllis's hat uses Abby's Hat template. The edge of the circle is gathered to fit her head and then a ruffle is sewn around the edge. A button is sewn to the center of the hat, and a bit of stuffing inside the hat helps it keep its shape. Eyelids cut from blue fabric let you know that Phyllis could use some tips on applying makeup.

Iris

The tiny flowers on Iris's purse and shoes are fingernail accessories found in the nail care section of a drug store. The loopy yarn used for her hair gives her that naturally curly look. Fusible web is ironed between two squares of fabric, and then a 6" circle is cut out for the hat brim. The fusible web gives weight to the hat and keeps the edges from fraying.

Kitty

A length of black ribbon creates a strap for Kitty's camera. The camera charm was found in the scrapbooking section of a craft store. The vast selection of scrapbooking embellishments is a great place to search for doll accessories. Kitty's jacket is made from fake fur, which is also added to her hat and boots.

Chef Caesar Selid

The Chef is made with Abby's body and Estelle's head and arms. Wool roving was needle felted to his head and face to create hair, eyebrows, and a moustache. An inkjet-printable fabric sheet was used to personalize his towel.

CHAPTER THREE

Estelle
16" Sitting Doll

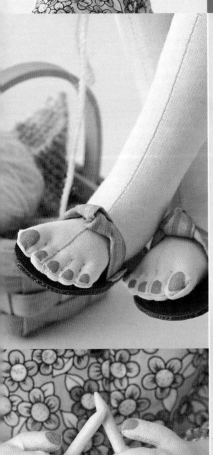

Materials

- ½ yard Kona Cotton for body
- ¼ yard fabric for blouse
- ¼ yard fabric for shorts
- 4" × 8" piece of imitation leather or vinyl for shoes
- 8" of 1"-wide (or wider) lace trim for bra
- 4" × 8" scrap of cotton print for shoe top
- 3 tiny buttons for blouse (In place of the tiny buttons, you could also use beads or small charms. Anything that is small enough to be in proportion would work.)
- 2 buttons ½" wide for shorts
- 8" length of ¼"-wide elastic for shorts
- Loosely twisted wool yarn or roving for hair (about 1 oz.) (Wool or wool blended with alpaca, llama, or goat can be used for the hair. Choose yarn that is loosely twisted or use roving. Roving has been cleaned and combed and is ready to spin into yarn. It can be purchased by the ounce.)
- 2 white pipe cleaners for fingers
- Polyester fiberfill
- Coordinating thread for sewing body and clothes
- Safety pin
- Strong quilting thread to sculpt face in color to match face
- Artist-quality watercolor pencils for painting face
- Eyelash bunches (You could omit the lashes and draw them instead [page 26].)
- 3" × 3" piece of fusible web for eyelids

Embellishments

The list of items for embellishing shows what was used for the project doll. If you choose a different theme you could come up with your own list of items that are made or purchased ready-made.

- ¼"-wide jump ring for finger ring
- 12" string of seed beads for beaded eyeglass holder (Instead of beads for the eyeglass holder, you could use string or ribbon.)
- 2½" eyeglasses (measured side to side)
- 2mm or 3mm beads for necklace, bracelet, earrings, and ring

- 10" length of ⅛"-wide dowel for knitting needles
- Scraps of yarn to fill basket
- 4" basket (or box)
- ½" claw hair clip
- Paint and textile medium to paint fingernails and toenails (See Resources on page 111.)

TEMPLATES REQUIRED

Find the template patterns beginning on page 96. Make templates following the instructions on page 13.

Head Front B, Head Back B, Body A, Arm C, Leg B, Breast, Ear, Blouse Front B, Blouse Back B, Blouse Sleeve B, Shorts Center Front, Shorts Back, Shorts Side Front, Shoe Sole B, Toe Sewing Guide, Eye, Eyelid

CONSTRUCTING THE BODY

Before you begin, review Chapter 1, The Cloth Doll: Basic Body Construction (pages 10–31). As you are sewing, you can refer back to Chapter 1 any time you feel you need additional direction. Read through all the pattern instructions before you begin.

Tracing, Sewing, and Cutting

1. Find the direction of stretch on the body fabric and draw an arrow at the edge of the fabric in the direction of the stretch to use as a guide (page 14).

2. Lay out the templates on 2 layers of fabric, with right sides together, matching the arrow on each template to the arrow you marked on the fabric, for Head Front B, Head Back B, Body A, Arm C, Leg B, and Breast.

3. Use a mechanical pencil to neatly trace around each template. Trace the leg, arm, and ear twice. Make your pencil lines just dark enough to see. If the lines are too dark, they may show through light-colored fabric. On each piece, identify the dashed sewing lines, the solid cutting lines, and the openings for turning and stuffing. Shorten the stitch length on your machine and use the smallest stitch when sewing around the fingers (page 16). Take your time and sew directly on the pencil lines.

4. Cut out each piece with a ⅛″ seam allowance. On the cutting lines that you did not sew, cut out directly on the pencil lines.

Stuffing the Body

1. Use turning tubes to turn the fingers right side out (page 17).

2. Wire the fingers (pages 17–18). Don't bend the fingers until after they are painted. Having the hand with all of the fingers outstretched is the perfect position for a manicure.

3. Finish sewing and stuffing the head (pages 19–29).

4. Turn the body right side out. Stuff the doll body through the opening in the neck. Make sure that there is ample stuffing in the neck so it doesn't wrinkle. The neck may seem long, but there needs to be enough to push up into the head to make it secure. Whipstitch the neck closed. This seam will be hidden when the head is attached.

5. Before you turn the legs, use the toe sewing guide (page 99) to trace the toes. This will give the toes a better shape for sculpting than sewing straight across. Line up the seams on the top and bottom of the foot. Trace the toe sewing guide, making sure to flip over the template on the second foot so you have a right and left foot. Sew on the traced line. Trim the seam allowance.

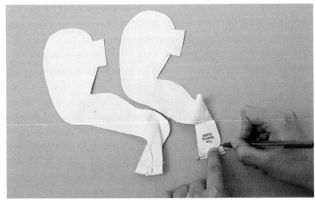

Mark foot using toe sewing guide.

6. Turn both legs right side out. Stuff each leg firmly from the toes up to the middle of the thigh. Stuff the rest of the thigh area so that it is soft. The top of the thigh will be wrapped around the side of the body, so it needs to be soft enough to manipulate.

Sculpting the Toes

Sculpting and painting is done before the limbs are attached.

1. Insert 4 pins in the end of the foot to mark the separation between the toes. The pins will help hold the thread in place as you sculpt. The big toe should be larger than the rest of the toes. Use a strong quilting thread in a color that closely matches the body fabric.

2. Anchor the thread at the seam on the underside of the foot. Sew 3 or 4 small stitches between each toe. The needle goes straight in the top of the foot and out the bottom of the foot. Take a small stitch and come back out on top so there are stitches on both sides of the foot.

Try to keep the stitches about the same size and in straight lines on the top and bottom of the foot for a neat appearance. End the thread where you began at the seam on the underside of the foot. Repeat for the second foot.

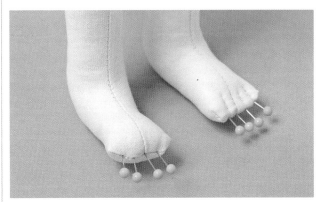

Mark toes with pins and stitch.

Painting the Toenails and Fingernails

Paint the toenails and fingernails the same color with a small paintbrush. I used acrylic paint. Liquitex acrylic paint and textile medium are shown in the photo on page 52 (see Resources, page 111). Add a textile medium to the paint to make it permanent. You will find textile medium sold next to acrylic paints in craft stores. The smallest bottle (2 fl. oz.) is more than you will need. Mix the medium with the paint according to the directions on the bottle. It takes very little paint for both the fingers and the toes. A dot of paint about the size of a dime is plenty. If the directions say to heat set, you can use a hair dryer.

Paint fingernails.

As an option, you could use the watercolor pencils that are used to paint the face. The pencils will glide easier on damp fabric. Use a paintbrush to wet the toe area before you begin. Outline the nails with a sharp pencil and then fill in the center.

Paint toenails.

Attaching the Legs and Arms

1. Attach the legs and arms using thread to match the body fabric. Pin the legs to the body, wrapping the thighs around the hips. The hips need to be in line so the doll will sit straight and balanced. Make sure the body is sitting straight and the shoulders are even. Starting at the top of the hip, use a ladder stitch to sew around the inside of the leg and back up to the hip.

2. Pin the arms to the body at the shoulders. Keep in mind what props the doll will be hold as you position the arms. Use a ladder stitch and sew around the arms.

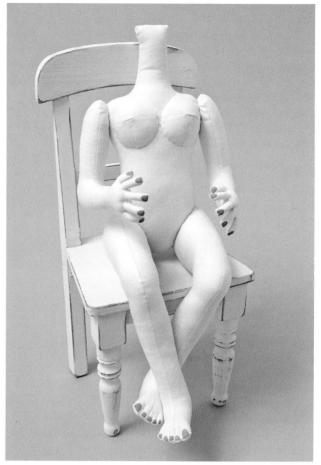

Attach legs and arms.

Making the Breasts and Bra

The breasts and bra are made in the same way as Abby's (pages 35–36).

DRESSING THE DOLL

Blouse

All the clothes have ¼" seam allowances included unless otherwise stated. It is best to have an iron handy and press open the seams of each garment as you sew.

1. Fold the blouse fabric in half with right sides together. Use the templates for Blouse Front B, Blouse Back B, and Blouse Sleeve B. The Blouse Back B and Blouse Sleeve B templates should be placed on the fold. Pin the templates to the fabric, and then trace and cut out.

2. With right sides together, pin the blouse fronts to the blouse back at the shoulders and sew.

3. Fold under the bottom edge of each sleeve ½" and sew.

4. With right sides together, pin the sleeves to the armholes of the blouse and sew.

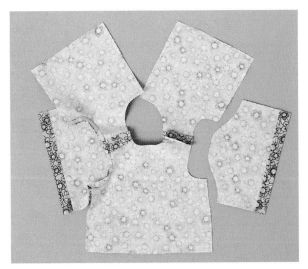

Blouse construction

5. Sew the underside of each sleeve and blouse side in a single seam. Turn the blouse right side out.

6. Fold under the bottom edge of the blouse ¼" and sew.

7. Fold under the edge of the neckline ¼" and sew.

8. Put the blouse on the doll. Fold under the raw edges at the front of the blouse. Sew 3 tiny buttons or beads to one side of the blouse. Use a ladder stitch to close the front opening of the blouse.

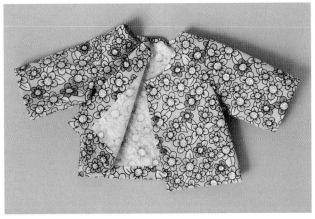

Finished blouse

Shorts

1. For the shorts, use the Shorts Center Front, Shorts Side Front, and Shorts Back templates. Lay out 2 layers of fabric with right sides together. Pin the templates to the fabric, and then trace and cut out.

2. With right sides together, sew the 2 back pieces together at the center back seam.

3. With right sides together, sew the 2 center front pieces together at the center front seam.

4. With right sides together, sew 1 side front piece to each side of the shorts center front.

5. With right sides together, pin the front to the back at the crotch and sew around the crotch seam.

6. Sew the front to the back at the side seams. Sew from the waist down about 5". Leave the bottom edges of the side seams open.

7. Fold under the waist of the shorts ¾". Sew around the waist ½" from the edge, forming a casing for the elastic. Stop the seam 1" from where you began to leave a hole for inserting the elastic.

8. Attach a safety pin to the end of an 8" length of ¼"-wide elastic. Insert the safety pin into the waist and work it all the way through the casing. Overlap the 2 ends of elastic ½" and sew together. Finish sewing the waist seam.

Insert elastic in waistband.

9. Try the shorts on the doll body. Fold under the shorts hem so that it is just above the knee. Pin. Fold open the seam allowance on the side seams. Sew around the bottom edges of the legs and up the side seams.

Fold hem and side seam allowances.

10. Turn right side out. Sew a ½″-wide button at the top of the opening in the side seam on each leg.

Add buttons.

Shoes

1. Cut 2 pieces of vinyl 4″ × 4″. Lay them with wrong sides together. Use the Shoe Sole B template to trace 2 soles on the right side of the vinyl.

NOTE

Wet the tip of a white watercolor pencil to trace on dark-colored vinyl. When you are finished, wipe off the lines with a damp sponge.

2. Using a coordinating thread color, sew around each sole.

3. Cut out each sole about ⅛″ from the stitched line.

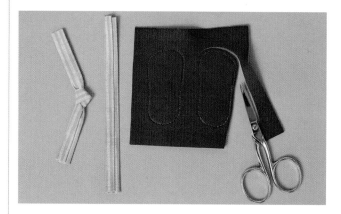

4. Cut 2 rectangles 1½″ × 5″ each from the accent fabric for the shoe top. Fold the long raw edges to the middle and then fold in half lengthwise so each piece measures approximately ¼″ × 5″. Tie a knot in the center of each.

5. Try a shoe on the doll to get the proper size. With the knot in the center, sew the strap to the shoe on the stitched line on each side of the sole. Trim excess fabric on each side of the shoe. Repeat for the other shoe. Put the shoes on the doll.

Add straps.

TIP

Instead of using an accent fabric for the strap, you could cut straps from the same vinyl used for the shoe soles. Maisie (page 59) has shoes with 3 straps, each cut ⅛″ wide.

Sculpting and Painting the Face

Refer to Chapter 1, beginning on page 10, for help in sculpting and painting the face, adding the eyelids and lashes, and attaching the head to the body.

Ears

1. Use the Ear template to trace 2 ears on doubled fabric.

2. Sew all the way around each ear with a very short stitch length.

3. Cut out the ears with a scant ⅛" seam allowance.

4. Lay out the ears so there is a right and left ear. Cut a slit in the back of each ear. Turn right side out.

Turning tubes are helpful to turn ears right side out.

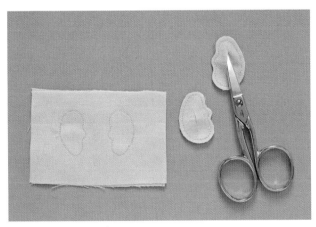

Trace, sew, cut out, and turn ears.

5. Stuff each ear slightly. Tuck a scrap of fabric into the hole to cover the opening.

6. Using a very short stitch length and sewing on the front side of the ear, outline the shape of the ear. Then sew a "C" shape in the center of the ear. The stitches will secure the scrap of fabric in the hole on the back of the ear, which will be hidden after the ears are attached.

7. Sew a bead to each earlobe for earrings.

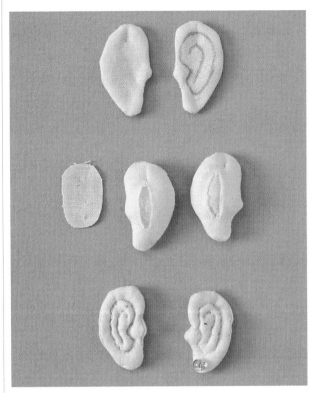

Ear construction

8. Sew the ears on the side seam of the head. The top of the ear should be even with the bottom edge of the eye.

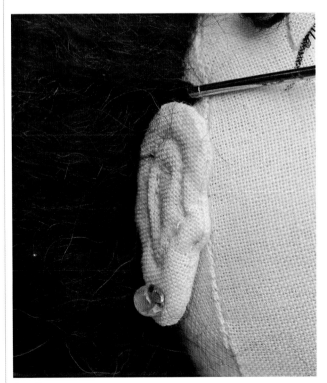

Attach ears.

CREATING THE HAIRSTYLE

Estelle's hair is made from a dark brown wool yarn blend that is 50% alpaca and 50% wool. Just a hint of a lighter color is added for highlights and a touch of white. Choose a loosely twisted yarn and a medium or fine felting needle.

The felting needles are very sharp and have barbs at the end. Felting is simple and fun; just keep your fingers out of the way. Lay the yarn on the stuffed doll head. In a quick motion, push the needle through the yarn and into the doll head. The barbs on the felting needle grab the fibers of the yarn and push them into the head, tangling them with the stuffing in the head.

1. Cut the yarn in 6″ lengths. Untwist the yarn.

2. Lay the yarn on the head in a starburst pattern from the crown toward the hairline.

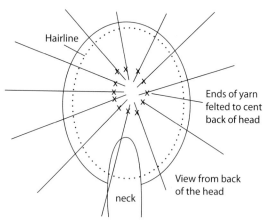

Felt yarn to center back and continue felting, radiating out to the hairline.

3. Push the felting needle quickly in and out to attach the ends of the yarn to the center of the back of the head. Mix in different yarn colors if you'd like to add some highlights to the hair.

Felt ends of wool to center of back of head.

4. Once all the yarn ends are attached to the head, create a smooth hairline. Felt around the head in a circle. The hairline frames the face, goes behind the ears, and covers the top of the neck, where it attaches to the back of the head. You can create a hairline guide with straight pins if you find it helpful. Try to keep the hairline in a smooth circle around the head.

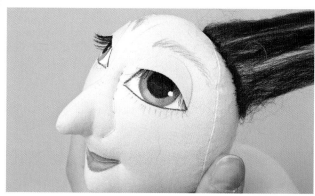

Create hairline.

5. Pull apart strands of yarn and create a messy ball of fibers. Use the felting needle to attach the ball of fibers to the top of the head, just above the hairline. This ball will help give the hairstyle some fullness.

Create ball of fibers.

6. Gather all the yarn around the hairball to the back of the head. Wrap the ends into a tight bun. Use the felting needle to secure the bun. Do not push the needle all the way into the doll's head. Push the needle in just deep enough to attach the bun to the ball of fibers underneath.

7. A few spiral curls are added to the bun and around the face. Wet a length of yarn. Wrap the yarn around a metal knitting needle (or the largest turning tube). Allow the curls to dry completely overnight or place them in a warm oven set at 200°.

8. Slide the curls off the knitting needle. Spray the curls with hair spray. Cut them into short lengths and use the felting needle to attach them to the hair. A tiny claw hair clip is attached to the bun.

Use felting needle to attach curls.

Felting the doll hair will give you more hairstyle options. It will allow you to make parts in the hair without the use of thread. Felt in a straight line to make a part in the hair. If you choose a style that hangs straight, give the doll a haircut to even up the ends, just as you would with any material used. You can also use hair spray to help keep the finished style neat. Use paper to cover up the doll's face before spraying.

EMBELLISHING THE DOLL

1. Place the glasses on the end of the doll's nose. String a 12″ length of seed beads and tie it to each side of the glasses. Instead of beads, you could use ribbon or string.

2. Create a 5″ string of beads on a length of thread for the necklace. Tie the string of beads around the doll's neck and cut off the ends of the thread. Make the bracelet the same way by creating a 3″ string of beads.

3. Open a ¼″ jump ring and slide on a single bead to make a ring for the doll's finger.

4. The knitting needles are made from a ⅛″-wide dowel. Cut a 10″-long dowel in half. Use a pencil sharpener to make a point on one end of each dowel.

5. Estelle's project was knitted on 2.75mm knitting needles using scraps of yarn. When the knitting is the length you desire, slide the stitches onto the ⅛″-wide dowels—half the stitches on each dowel. Use an off-white or clear thread to attach the knitting to the palm of each hand.

Attach knitting to hands.

6. Fill a 4″ basket with balls of yarn.

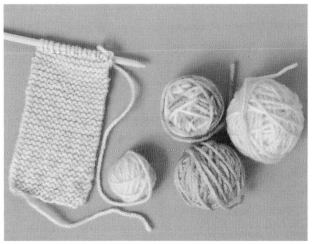

Yarn embellishments

Lorna

A 3″ embroidery hoop is used for Lorna's quilt project. If you are a quilter, this is a fabulous way to display a miniature quilt block. Tiny wooden thread spools from the craft store are wrapped with thread to match her project. A button in the shape of scissors is the perfect finishing touch for her basket.

Maisie

The cover of Maisie's book was made on the computer and printed on copy paper. The cover was then glued to cardboard, and pages were added to create a book. A store-bought felt hat was embellished with silk flowers, ribbon, and feathers that are glued in place. A papier-mâché box can be covered with paper or painted for a hat box.

CHAPTER FOUR

Jilly

16″ Doll Sitting Cross-Legged

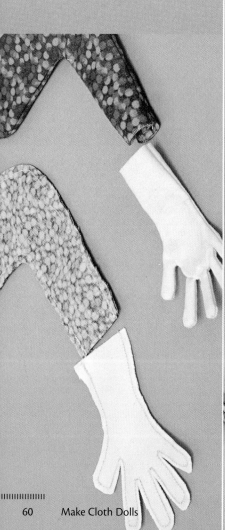

Materials

- ½ yard Kona Cotton for body
- ¼ yard fabric for blouse
- ¼ yard fabric for arms, blouse tie, shoe tops, and shoe strap
- ¼ yard fabric for shorts
- 3 tiny buttons for blouse (In place of the tiny buttons, you could also use beads or small charms. Anything that is small enough to be in proportion would work.)
- 4 tiny buttons for shoes
- 8" length of ¼"-wide elastic for shorts waist
- 8" length of ½"-wide trim for wrists
- 18" length of ½"- to ¾"-wide trim for shorts
- 16" length of ¼"-wide ribbon for hair tie
- ¼ skein of lumpy and fuzzy yarn for hair
- 2 white pipe cleaners for fingers
- Polyester fiberfill
- Coordinating thread for sewing
- Safety pin
- Strong quilting thread to sculpt face in color to match face
- Artist-quality watercolor pencils for painting face
- Eyelash bunches (You could omit the lashes and draw them instead [page 26].)
- 4" × 9" piece of fusible web for eyelids, shoe tops, and shoe straps
- 4" × 8" piece of imitation leather or vinyl for shoe soles

Embellishments

The list of items for embellishing shows what was used for the project doll. If you choose a different theme you could come up with your own list of items that are made or purchased ready-made. The scrapbooking items were made on the computer and printed on cardstock.

- Seed beads for necklace, bracelet, and earrings
- ⅛"-wide dowel for pencils
- Acrylic paints for pencils
- 8½" × 11" sheet of cardstock for pencil box, supply box, and books
- 3" × 4" piece of vinyl for journal

TEMPLATES REQUIRED

Find the template patterns beginning on page 96. Make templates following the instructions on page 13.

Head Front C, Head Back B, Body A, Arm A, Hand A, Leg B, Leg C, Ear, Blouse Front C, Blouse Back C, Sleeve C, Shorts Center Front, Shorts Back, Shorts Side Front, Shoe Sole B, Shoe Top C, Shoe Strap, Pencil Box, Scrapbooking Supplies, Eye, Eyelid

CONSTRUCTING THE BODY

Before you begin, review Chapter 1, The Cloth Doll: Basic Body Construction (pages 10–31). As you are sewing, you can refer back to Chapter 1 any time you feel you need additional direction. Read through all the pattern instructions before you begin.

Tracing, Sewing, and Cutting

1. Find the direction of stretch on the body fabric and draw an arrow at the edge of the fabric in the direction of the stretch to use as a guide (page 14).

2. Lay out the templates Head Front C, Head Back B, Body A, Hand A, Leg B, and Leg C on 2 layers of fabric, right sides together, matching the arrow on each template to the arrow you marked on the fabric.

3. Use a mechanical pencil to neatly trace around each template. Trace the hand twice. Make the pencil lines just dark enough to see. If the lines are too dark, they may show through light-colored fabric. On each piece, identify the dashed sewing lines, the solid cutting lines, and the openings for turning and stuffing. Shorten the stitch length on your machine and use the smallest stitch when sewing around the fingers. Take your time and sew directly on the pencil lines.

4. Cut out each piece with a ⅛" seam allowance. The cutting lines that you did not sew should be cut out directly on the pencil lines.

Stuffing the Body

1. Use turning tubes to turn the fingers right side out (page 17).

2. Wire the fingers (pages 17–18).

3. Follow the directions on pages 19–31 (Constructing the Head) to finish sewing and stuffing the head and to create the face.

4. Make the ears (page 55).

5. Turn the body right side out. Stuff the doll body through the opening in the neck. Make sure that there is ample stuffing in the neck so it doesn't wrinkle. The neck may seem long, but there needs to be enough to push up into the head to make it secure. Whipstitch the neck closed. This seam will be hidden when the head is attached.

6. Open the toe, line up the seams so one is on top of the foot and the other is on the bottom, and then sew across the toes. Repeat for the other foot. Turn both legs right side out.

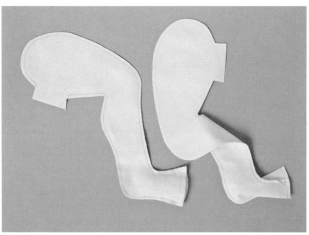

Align toe seams and sew across toes.

7. Stuff each leg firmly from the toes up to the middle of the thigh. Stuff the rest of the thigh area so that it is soft. The top of the thigh will be wrapped around the side of the body, so it needs to be soft enough to manipulate.

Attaching the Legs

1. Pin the legs to the body, wrapping the thighs around the hips. One leg is bent more than the other. The legs are bent at different angles, so the placement on the hip won't be exactly the same. It won't be noticeable once the shorts are put on. The most important thing is to get the body sitting straight and balanced.

2. Starting at the top of the hip, use a ladder stitch to sew around the inside of the leg and back up to the hip. Attach the legs using thread to match the body fabric.

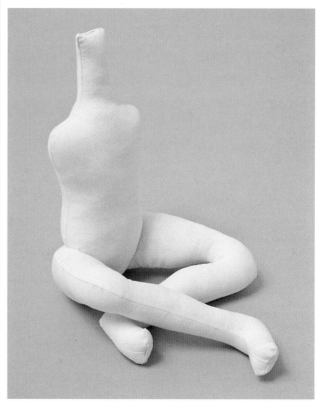

Position and attach legs.

Making the Arms and Hands

Making the hand separate from the arm allows you to turn the wrist in any position. Mallory (page 69) has her left hand positioned with the palm up to hold her hot fudge sundae. This method also gives a layered look, as if the doll is wearing 2 shirts.

1. The arms are made from a cotton print fabric, using the Arm A template. Find the direction of stretch on the arm fabric. Draw an arrow at the edge of the fabric in the direction of the stretch to use as a guide.

2. Lay out the arm template on 2 layers of fabric, right sides together, matching the arrow on the template to the arrow you marked on the fabric. Use a mechanical pencil to neatly trace around the template twice. Identify the dashed sewing lines and the solid cutting lines. Pin the fabric layers together.

3. Sew around each arm.

4. Cut out each arm with a ⅛" seam allowance. Turn the arms right side out and stuff firmly.

5. Fold under the raw edges of fabric ½" at the wrist on each arm and hand. Decide what you will put in the hands, so that you can position them accordingly. Hold something similar in your own hand to study the position of your wrist. Pin the hands to the arms. Make sure the thumb position is correct for the right and left hands. Ladder stitch the hands to the arms. Add a little more stuffing before closing the ladder stitch to make sure the wrists are firm. Wait to bend the fingers into position until later.

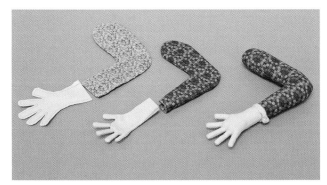

Hand/arm construction

6. Cut a 2½" length of trim for each wrist. Wrap the trim around the wrist so that it covers the seam where the arm and hand join. Choose a thread color to match the trim so the stitches are not seen. Sew the trim on with tiny stitches around the wrist.

7. Pin the arms to the body. Consider what the doll will be holding in her hands as you position the arms. Ladder stitch the arms to the body using thread that matches the arm fabric.

DRESSING THE DOLL

All the clothes have ¼" seam allowances included unless otherwise stated. It is best to have an iron handy and press open the seams of each garment as you sew.

Shorts

1. For the shorts, use the Shorts Center Front, Shorts Side Front, and Shorts Back templates. Lay out 2 layers of fabric with right sides together. Pin the templates to the fabric and cut out.

2. With right sides together, sew the 2 back pieces together at the center back seam.

3. With right sides together, sew the 2 center front pieces together at the center front seam.

4. With right sides together, sew 1 side piece to each side of the shorts center front.

5. With right sides together, pin the front to the back at the crotch and sew around the crotch seam.

6. Place the trim on the right side of the shorts ½" above the bottom edge of each leg. The ruffled trim should lie with the ruffled edge toward the waist. Sew the trim to each shorts leg. Press the hem under so the trim hangs down and stitch across the hem.

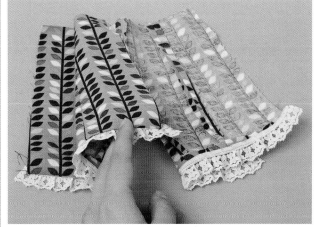

Add trim.

7. Match up the bottom edges of the shorts legs and sew the shorts side front to the back at the side seams.

8. Fold under the waist of the shorts ¾″. Sew around the waist ½″ from the edge, forming a casing for the elastic. Stop the seam 1″ from where you began to leave a hole for inserting the elastic.

9. Attach a safety pin to the end of an 8″ length of ¼″-wide elastic. Insert the safety pin into the waist and work it all the way through the casing. Overlap the 2 ends of elastic ½″ and sew together. Finish sewing the waist seam. Put the shorts on the doll.

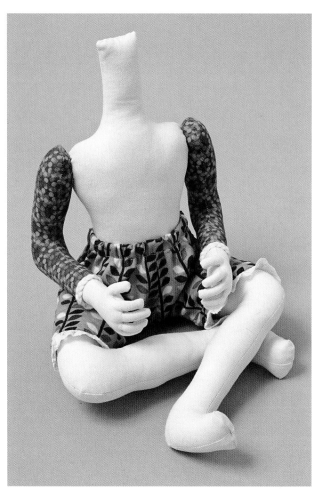

Finished shorts on doll

Blouse

1. Fold the blouse fabric in half with right sides together. Use the templates Blouse Front C, Blouse Back C, and Sleeve C. Blouse Front C and Sleeve C should be placed on the fold. Pin the templates to the fabric, and then trace and cut out. The bottom of the blouse does not have a template. Cut a rectangle 3″ × 18″.

2. With right sides together, pin the blouse fronts to the blouse back at the shoulders and sew.

3. Fold under the neckline a scant ¼″ and sew.

4. Fold under the bottom edge of each sleeve ¼″ and sew a gathering stitch close to the edge of the hem.

5. Sew a gathering stitch at the top of the sleeve as shown on the template pattern.

6. With right sides together, pin the sleeve to the armhole of the blouse, pulling the threads to gather the sleeve so it fits the armhole. Sew around the armhole. The bottom edge of the sleeve is gathered after the blouse is put together.

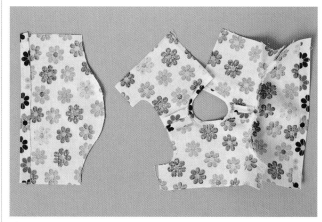

Blouse construction

7. Sew the underside of each sleeve and the blouse side in a single seam. Turn the blouse right side out.

8. Try the blouse on the doll with the opening at the back. Fold under the fabric at the back opening so that the edges overlap. Sew 3 tiny buttons on one side.

9. Sew a ¼″ hem on one 18″ side and both 3″ sides of the rectangle you cut for the blouse bottom. On the remaining 18″ side, sew a gathering stitch. The gathered edge will be the waistline of the blouse.

10. Pull the threads to gather the rectangle until it fits the blouse top and pin in place. Sew around the waist of the blouse.

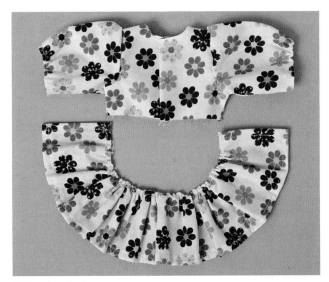

Add gathered edge.

11. Put the blouse on the doll with the opening at the back. Ladder stitch the blouse closed.

12. Use the same fabric that was used on the arms to make a tie. Cut a rectangle 1″ × 22″. With right sides together, fold the tie in half lengthwise. Sew the tie at each short end and down the long edge, leaving a hole in the middle to turn it right side out.

13. Turn the tie right side out. (You can use the finger turning tubes.) Press. Tie in a bow around the doll's waist.

Shoes

1. Stack 2 pieces of vinyl 4″ × 4″ wrong sides together. Use the Shoe Sole B template to trace 2 soles on the right side of the vinyl.

> **NOTE**
> Wet the tip of a white watercolor pencil, and you can trace on dark vinyl. When you are finished, wipe off the lines with a damp sponge.

Trace soles.

2. Use a coordinating thread color and sew around the traced line on each sole.

3. Cut out each sole with a ⅛″ seam allowance.

4. Cut 2 pieces of shoe top fabric and 1 piece of fusible web, each 4″ × 6″. Stack them with the fusible web in the middle and the right sides of the fabric facing out. Iron the fabric so the fusible web joins the 2 fabrics as one. It will also keep the fabric edges from fraying when they are cut.

5. Cut 2 each of the templates Shoe Top C and Shoe Strap C from the fused fabric.

6. Sew a dart in the toe of each shoe top, as shown on the template pattern.

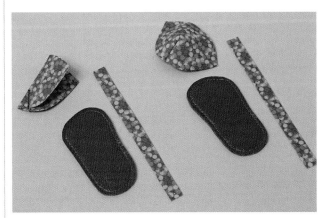

Shoe construction

7. Using a zigzag or satin stitch, sew the shoe top to the shoe sole.

8. Try the shoe on the doll's foot so you can test for the length of the strap.

9. Sew a tiny button on each side of the shoe top to hold the strap in place. Put the shoes on the doll.

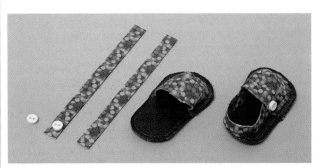

Add straps.

Finished shoe

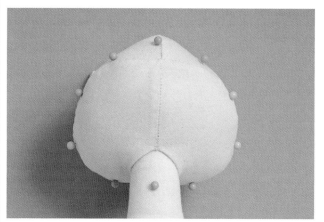

Add straight pins as sewing guide for hairline.

ATTACHING THE HEAD

After the body is finished and dressed, construct the head and paint the face (pages 19–29). Now it is time to attach the head. Push the neck into the stuffing hole of the head. If you can't get the neck far enough into the head to be secure, remove a bit of the stuffing. Make sure the chin is down far enough so that the doll is not looking up. Pin the head to the neck to hold it in place as you sew. Use the ladder stitch to sew the head to the neck. You want the stitches to be hidden. Knot off the thread on the back of the neck, where it will be hidden by the hair.

CREATING THE HAIRSTYLE

Jilly's hair is made from a textured, frizzy yarn. The textured yarns look nice at the hairline, and the individual strands will blend together seamlessly. Subtle color variations in the yarn help add texture to the overall look. Look beyond the smooth yarns when you choose hair material.

1. Cut yarn in 14" lengths.

2. Choose a thread color that will disappear into the yarn. Thread a curved needle with a long but manageable length of thread. You can start new lengths of thread as needed.

3. Use straight pins to define the hairline. Frame the face, go behind the ears, and across the top of the neck.

4. Pick up a piece of yarn in the center. Lay it across the head so the center of the yarn is on the hairline. Stitch the yarn to the head. Lay the next piece of yarn up against the first one and take a stitch at the hairline. Take the pins out as you come to them. Continue until you have gone all the way around the head.

Stitch hair.

5. Hold the doll upside down and comb through the yarn with your fingers. Grab the yarn in a ponytail that is centered on top of the head. Tie the ponytail with a 16″ length of ¼″-wide ribbon.

6. Trim the ends of the ponytail to even up the strands.

Finished hair

EMBELLISHING THE DOLL

1. String a 7″ strand of seed beads for the necklace. Put the strand around the neck and tie the thread ends in a knot. Pull the ends of the thread through a few beads and cut off. Repeat for the bracelet, using a 3″ strand of beads.

2. The pencil in Jilly's hand is a ⅛″-wide dowel cut 2½″ long. Use a small pencil sharpener to make a point on one end of the dowel. Use acrylic paints in yellow, gray, silver, and brown to paint the pencil. Bend the fingers to make the doll hold the pencil in her hand. Clear thread is used to secure the pencil to the hand.

3. Make the pencils in the box in the same way. Cut several pencils that are 2″ long from a ⅛″-wide dowel. Sharpen one end of each 2″ dowel piece. Paint each pencil a different color. Use the template for the pencil box and trace it onto cardstock. Cut a hole in the box to show off the pencils. Cut out the pencil box template (page 105). Fold on the dashed lines and glue the flaps. Use your computer and printer to make a label for the box. You could also use decorative paper to make a box.

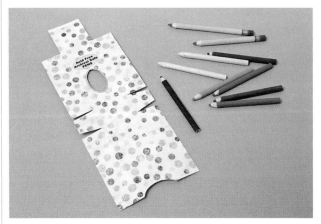

Pencil box construction

4. Make the journal in Jilly's hand from a 2¼″ × 3″ piece of vinyl. Cut a rectangle 2″ by 3″ and a strap ¼″ × 2″ from vinyl. Fold the vinyl in half so the book is 2″ tall by 1½″ wide. Fold a few pieces of scrap paper and glue them inside the book. Wrap the strap around the opening of the book. Sew a tiny button or bead on the end of the strap. Push the needle through the entire book and back out to the button to hold the book closed. Glue a label to the front of the book. Use clear thread to sew the book to the palm of the hand. Bend the fingers to hold the book.

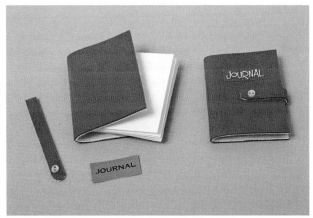

Journal construction

Finished journal

5. Make the scrapbooking supply box from cardstock using the Scrapbooking Supply Box template (page 104). Trace around the template and cut out. Fold on the dashed lines and glue the flaps. Thread embroidery floss on a needle, knot the end, and push the needle through the ends of the box to create handles. Fill the box with colored papers with labels for stickers, cards, photo corners, and paper. Make a sheet of tiny images labeled "stickers" that resemble sheets of stickers. Cut tiny tags and tie thread to the ends.

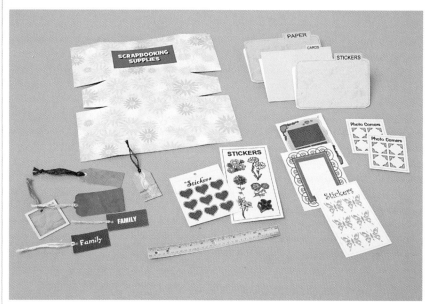

Embellishments

6. Make book covers using 2″ × 4″ pieces of cardstock. Glue scrap paper inside for pages. Use your computer to print book titles or write on decorative paper with a marker to help promote the theme.

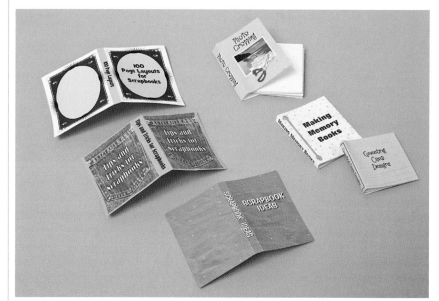

Book construction

Mallory

A tasting spoon from the ice cream store and a condiment cup from a restaurant are the perfect size for this doll. The ice cream and cherry are balls of oven-baked clay. Green thread knotted at the end creates a stem for the cherry. Shiny puff paint looks like fudge and whipped cream good enough to eat. A toothpick cut into tiny bits is sprinkled over the paint while it is still wet to look like nuts.

CHAPTER FIVE

EMILY ANN and Her Doll
22″ Button-Jointed Rag Doll with a 9″ Companion Doll

Materials for Body (Both Dolls)

- ⅓ yard Kona Cotton for bodies
- ¼ yard striped fabric for legs (Keep in mind when choosing a fabric for the legs that the more complex the stripe or design is, the more patience and fabric it will take to match up the stripes when you sew. If you choose a stripe for the leg fabric, the direction of the stripe will take precedence over the direction of the stretch in the fabric. Take your time lining up the stripes on the leg seams. If the stripe doesn't match up, it will be very noticeable. If you choose an uneven stripe or other uneven design for the legs, it can be very difficult to match up the design on the seams, so keep this in mind when choosing leg fabric. Don't be afraid to stray away from the stripes and consider dots or other designs.)
- 2 ¾"-wide buttons or snaps for Emily Ann's eyes (The eye buttons may be simple or elaborate, with 2 holes, 4 holes, or a shank.)
- 2 ¼"-wide buttons or snaps for small doll's eyes
- 8 2-hole buttons for elbows and knees (½" to ¾" wide). The joint will move easier with a 2-hole button than it will with a 4-hole button.
- 4 2-hole buttons to attach arms and legs (½" to ¾" wide)
- 1 skein textured yarn for Emily Ann's hair. Lumpy, bumpy yarns are so much more interesting than smooth yarns. Specialty yarns come in more colors and textures than you can imagine. Choosing just the right yarn for the hair is another chance for you to make this doll your own. First consider the colors in the fabrics that you used. Take some fabric samples with you when picking out the yarn so you can choose a hair color that will fit well with the color palette of the doll. Next is the texture. I couldn't begin to name all the choices available. After looking at the choices, smooth yarn seems quite boring. If you do find a smooth yarn that you want to use because the color is perfect, try mixing in another yarn with it to add texture. Two of the dolls in the gallery (pages 91 and 95) have shoelace yarn for hair. It gives the look of fabric strips without all the fraying edges.
- 2 skeins embroidery floss (or yarn) for small doll's hair
- Polyester fiberfill

- 2 white pipe cleaners for Emily Ann's fingers
- Coordinating thread for sewing
- Safety pin
- Quilting thread in color to match doll head and body
- 1" needle to attach limbs and head and sculpt mouth
- Artist-quality paintbrush and watercolor pencils for painting face—white for eyes; black or brown for lashes and eyebrows; and red, pink, or peach for mouth and cheeks. The colors you choose for the face depend on the look you're going for and the colors in the fabrics you choose for the clothes.

Materials for Clothes (Both Dolls)

- ⅓ yard cotton print for Emily Ann's dress
- 8" × 12" piece of cotton print for small doll's dress
- ¼ yard cotton print for Emily Ann's dress ruffles and small doll's apron
- 5" × 25" strip of cotton print for edging detail on Emily Ann's dress (shown in dark rose)
- ¼ yard muslin for both dolls' pantaloons
- 24" of ½"-wide trim for small doll's dress and pantaloons. You can add or omit trims and ruffles on any part of Emily Ann's dress. If you don't want to make the ruffles for the bottom edge of the skirt or neckline of the dress, you could use purchased trims instead. The bottom edge of the skirt would require ¾ yard of a pregathered 2"-wide ruffle. If you choose a trim that you will gather yourself, then you would need 1½ to 2 yards, depending on the fullness you prefer. The finished neck of the dress is 7½", requiring ¼ yard of a pregathered 1"-wide ruffle or ½ yard if you choose a trim that you will gather. Some of the gallery dolls have pregathered lace for the neckline that is sewn down instead of standing up like the ruffle on Emily Ann's dress.
- 16" of 1"-wide trim for Emily Ann's pantaloons
- 10" of ¼"-wide ribbon for small doll's hair bow
- 28" of ¼"-wide ribbon to tie around Emily Ann's dress sleeves
- 1 yard of 1"-wide ribbon to tie around waist of Emily Ann's dress

- 6" × 8" piece of imitation leather or vinyl for Emily Ann's shoes. I can usually find pieces of vinyl in the remnant or discount bin, so make sure you look there first.

- 1 white knee-high sock for Emily Ann's socks. Two pairs of socks can be made from one knee-high sock. You could also use girls' tights or trouser socks. I like to buy a variety pack of knee-highs at the dollar store, so I always have several colors on hand.

- 9" of ¼"-wide elastic for Emily Ann's pantaloons

- 3 tiny round buttons for Emily Ann's dress back

- 4 heart buttons ¼"-wide—1 for each doll's neck trim and 2 for Emily Ann's shoes. Tiny heart buttons are used on the strap of each shoe. You could also use beads, charms, or anything that is small enough.

- Purchased hat with 3½" head opening

Emily Ann

TEMPLATES REQUIRED

Find the template patterns beginning on page 104. Make templates following the instructions on page 13.

Use all the templates with an "Emily Ann" label.

CONSTRUCTING EMILY ANN'S BODY

Before you begin, review Chapter 1, The Cloth Doll: Basic Body Construction (pages 10–31). As you are sewing, you can refer back to Chapter 1 any time you feel you need additional direction. Read through the instructions before you begin. Make sure to read Perfect Fingers Every Time in Chapter 1 (page 16) for additional details on constructing the fingers. Even though the arm templates may be different from pattern to pattern, the steps for creating the fingers are the same.

Tracing, Sewing, and Cutting

1. Find the direction of stretch on the body fabric and draw an arrow at the edge of the fabric in the direction of the stretch to use as a guide (page 14).

2. Lay out the templates on 2 layers of fabric, right sides together, following the stretch arrows, for the upper arms, lower arms, body, head front, head back, and arm tabs.

3. Use a mechanical pencil to neatly trace around each template. Notice that the lower arm template has a large dot to show where the seam begins. Above the dot is where the arm tab is attached after the arm is cut out. Make a mark on the fabric at each dot. Do not sew above the dots yet.

4. Identify the sewing lines, the cutting lines, and the openings for turning and stuffing for each body piece. Notice that the templates show a dashed line for sewing and a solid line for cutting. Pin the fabric together. Shorten the stitch length on your machine, making sure to use the smallest stitch when sewing around the fingers. Sew on each sewing line with thread to match the fabric. If you are having trouble seeing the pencil line as you sew, try using a clear or open-toe presser foot. Take your time sewing so you can sew directly on the pencil lines.

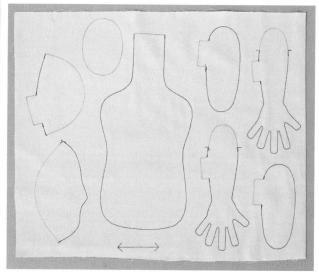

Note that top of the the lower arm is not sewn until tabs are added.

5. Cut out each sewn piece with a ⅛" seam allowance. Take special care when cutting out the fingers. The solid cutting lines are cut out on the pencil lines. The top of the lower arm shows a sewing line where the tab will be attached, so make sure to cut it out with a ¼" seam allowance.

Stuffing the Body

1. Turn the body right side out and stuff firmly.

The neck, wrists, and ankles tend to be areas that will be weak if not stuffed firmly. A firmly stuffed neck will hold the head up without creasing or bending.

2. Whipstitch the neck closed. The neck will be tucked up inside the head, so the stitches on the neck will not be visible on the finished doll.

The finger turning tubes can also be used for turning all the body pieces.

Making Button-Jointed Arms

1. Open the tab on the lower arm by folding one side down. Pin the tab to the arm with right sides together. The marks you made from the large dots on the template are the guides to show where the tab seam begins. Beginning at one dot and ending at the other, stitch around one side of the tab (shown below in blue thread), then flip the arm over and sew around the other side of the tab (shown below in red thread).

One side of tab is sewn with blue thread and other side sewn in red for clarity.

2. Turn the upper and lower arms right side out.

3. Cut 10 pieces of white pipe cleaner 1½˝ long. Bend over the sharp ends of the wire with pliers, so they won't poke through the fabric. Add the wire to the fingers and stuff as

described in Perfect Fingers Every Time (pages 16–18). The tabs are not stuffed, so put a straight pin at the opening of each tab to block the stuffing. Stuff the upper and lower arms firmly. Use a ladder stitch (page 9) to close the stuffing holes. Bend each finger around a pencil to get a nice curve in it.

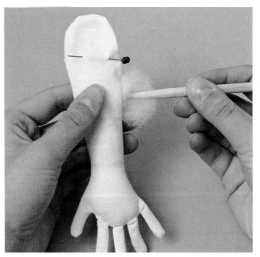

Stuff arms firmly.

4. Insert the end of the upper arm between the tabs on the lower arm. Position the stuffing hole on the upper arm closer to the shoulder and at the underside on the back of the arm. It looks neater to have this seam at the back of the arm rather than having it more visible at the front of the arm. Use a strong quilting thread to attach the buttons to the arms. Pin the tabs to each side of the upper arm to hold them in place while you sew. Use a needle that is long enough to go through the entire elbow, so you won't be poking and searching for the buttonhole on the other side. Sew back and forth from button to button 3 or 4 times and then knot the thread, hiding it behind the tab.

Making Button-Jointed Legs

The button joints at the knees will be constructed in the same manner as the elbow joints. The seam on the front of the lower leg will be the most visible part of the leg. Take your time and use many pins to match the stripes before you sew.

1. With right sides together, carefully line up the stripes and pin in place. Trace around the templates for the upper leg, lower leg, and leg tabs with a mechanical pencil. Notice that the templates show a dashed line for sewing and a solid line for cutting. The lower leg template has a large dot to show where the seam begins. Above the dot is where the leg tab is attached after the leg is cut out. Make a mark on the fabric at each dot. Do not sew above and between the dots yet. Sew the upper leg on the pencil line, leaving the opening for turning and stuffing. Sew the lower leg from the large dot at the tab to the toe on each side of the leg. The toe will be open for turning and stuffing. Cut along the seams with a ⅛" seam allowance. The pencil line at the toe is a cutting line. The top of the leg shows a sewing line where the tab will be attached, so make sure to cut it out with a ¼" seam allowance.

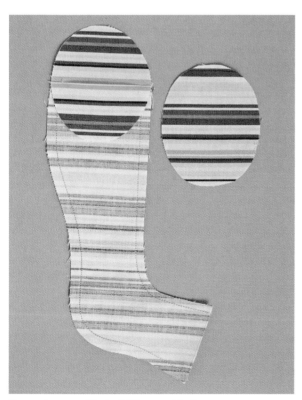

Open tab at top of leg by folding one side down.

2. Pin the circle tab in place with right sides together. Sew around the tab, just as you did with the arm. The marks that you made from the large dots on the template are the guides to show where the tab seam begins and ends. Sew around one side of the tab, then flip over the leg, and sew around the other side of the tab.

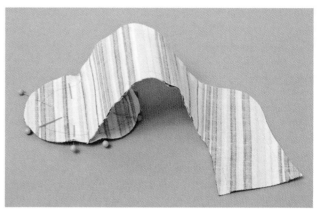

Pin circle tab in place.

3. Turn all leg pieces right side out. Stuff the upper leg firmly and sew the opening closed with a ladder stitch. The tabs are not stuffed on the lower leg, so put a straight pin at the opening of each tab to block out the stuffing. Stuff the lower leg firmly and use a whipstitch to close the toes.

Stuff legs and stitch opening closed.

4. Insert the end of the upper leg between the tabs on the lower leg. Position the stuffing hole on the upper leg closer to the hip and at the underside on the back of the leg. Use a strong quilting thread to attach the buttons to the knee joint. Pin the tabs to each side of the upper leg to hold them in place while you sew. Use a needle that is long enough to go through the entire knee so that you won't be poking and searching for the buttonhole on the other side. Sew back and forth from button to button 3 or 4 times and then knot the thread, hiding it behind the tab.

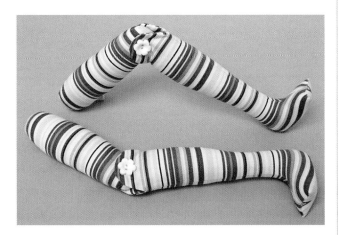

Attaching the Arms and Legs

The legs and arms are attached with buttons, so they move like elbows and knees. You can see the elbows and knees, so it is important to use matching buttons. However, the shoulders and hips will be covered by clothes, so you could use up any mismatched buttons you have on hand. If the buttons you choose have 4 holes, sew through only 2 of the holes for ease of movement.

1. Pin the arms to the body at the shoulders.

2. Use a strong quilting thread with a 7″ needle and sew back and forth from button to button through the body 4 or 5 times. Make sure to pull the slack out of the thread each time you pull the thread through the body. Tie off the thread at the button, not on the fabric. The knot may pull through the fabric, but the button will hold it securely. Repeat this process for the legs.

Using a 7″ needle allows you to direct the needle straight through the body and come out at the buttonhole.

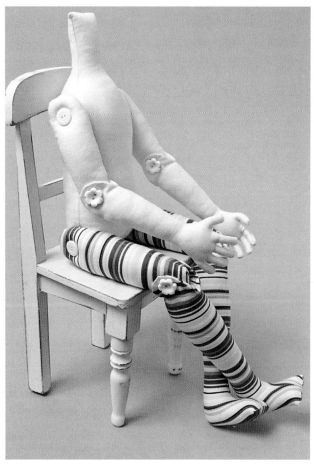

Pin and stitch arms and legs to body.

Making the Head

1. Open the head pieces and pin them with right sides together, lining up the center seam at the chin and forehead. As shown in detail in Chapter 1 (page 19), use many pins, so that you don't stretch or ease the fabric as you sew. The opening for turning and stuffing will be where the neck connects to the head. Make sure the head front (the side with the nose) is not upside down. Sew around the head with a ⅛″ seam allowance.

2. Turn the head right side out and stuff firmly. I attach the head to the body after the doll is dressed. The head can get in the way, and it is easier to dress the doll without it. The hair will be added after the head is attached.

Creating the Face

If you've never used watercolor pencils on fabric, you may want to make an extra head for practice. Keep the practice head so you can see the colors on the fabric for reference later. As you experiment, you will find that some colors bleed easily, while others don't bleed at all.

1. Use a paintbrush to wet the entire face up to the side seams.

NOTE

If the fabric is too wet, the colors may bleed. If the fabric is too dry, the colors won't blend nicely. The fabric should feel damp to the touch. The fabric will dry quickly, so if the head is too wet, simply wait a few minutes.

2. Pin the buttons to the face and then trace around them with a white pencil. Remove the buttons and color in the circles slightly larger than the buttons with white.

3. With a light touch, use the side of the pencil to rub some color on the cheeks, then blend and soften the color with a paintbrush. If you want more color on the cheeks, repeat the process. If there is too much color, you can blend some away with the paintbrush. It is always easier to add more than to blend some away. Keep in mind that the color will lighten up just a bit as it dries.

4. Draw a small heart for the mouth in reds or pinks, centered on the seam in the face. Draw the heart with a dark pink and then color in the center with a medium pink.

5. Add eyelashes and eyebrows with black or brown watercolor pencils.

Paint facial features.

NOTE

If you want to add more detail to the mouth, you could add a smile line. Emily Ann does not have a smile line, but you will notice that many of the other rag dolls in the gallery (pages 86–95) do. Thread a long needle with quilting thread and knot the end. Anchor the thread on the center seam at the back of the head above the stuffing hole. Stick the needle through the head so it comes out next to the heart (mouth). Take a long stitch away from the heart toward the cheek to form the smile. Go back through the head and anchor the thread where you began. The more tension you put on the stitch, the deeper the indentation of the smile. Repeat for the other side of the mouth.

6. Attach the button eyes with quilting thread. Anchor the thread on the center seam at the back of the head. Sew the buttons in the centers of the white circles and end the thread at the back of the head. The tighter you pull the thread, the deeper the buttons will be set in the face. Use your finger to push in the button as you pull the thread.

NOTE

If the button has a shank on the back instead of holes, it may not lie flat on the face. Use a seam ripper to poke a small hole in the center of the white circle. Push the shank into the hole, allowing the button to lie flat on the face.

TIP

Adding a small dot of white acrylic paint to each button will help the eyes come to life.

Set the head aside for now. After the doll is dressed, the head is attached and the hair is added.

DRESSING EMILY ANN

Pantaloons

1. Trace and cut out the pantaloons and cut a 14″ piece of 1″-wide lace or trim for the legs and a 9″ piece of ¼″-wide elastic for the waist.

2. With right sides together, sew the center seam on the front and back of the pantaloons.

3. Pin the front to the back and sew around the inside of both legs and the crotch in a single seam.

4. Open each leg and pin the lace to the bottom edges of the pantaloons, with right sides together, and sew. Iron the seam. The trim is easier to attach to the pantaloons before you sew the side seam because the leg opening is small.

5. Sew the side seams down each leg.

6. Fold under the waist ¾″. Sew around the waist ½″ from the top edge and stop 1″ from where you began to leave an opening for the elastic. Attach a safety pin to the end of the elastic. Use the safety pin to guide the elastic around the waist. Overlap the ends of the elastic ½″ and sew together. Sew the 1″ hole closed on the waist.

7. Put the pantaloons on the doll.

Pantaloons

NOTE

There are several options for finishing the pantaloons. If you choose to omit the lace, hem the bottom edge of each leg before you sew the side seams. You could also gather each leg 1″ from the bottom edge. Gather the leg with embroidery floss and knot or simply tie a length of ribbon around each leg. You could also add a decorative stitch in a contrasting thread to the edge of each pantaloon leg.

Dress

1. Fold the dress fabric with right sides together. Trace around the templates and cut out the dress front, back, and sleeves. Cut ¾ yard of 1″-wide ribbon to tie around the waist and two lengths 9″ of ¼″-wide ribbon to tie around the sleeves. Use a yardstick and a pencil to draw the rectangles noted below on the wrong side of the fabric and then cut them out. If you are a quilter and you have acrylic quilting rulers and a rotary cutter, you could make quick work of cutting out the rectangles. Cut out the rectangles as follows:

- Cut 1 rectangle 4½″ × 24″ from the dress fabric for the skirt.
- Cut 1 strip 3″ × 45″ for the skirt ruffle.

- Cut 1 strip 2″ × 16″ for the ruffle at the neck.

- Cut 2 strips 2″ × 8″ for the sleeve edging (shown in dark rose on the project doll).

- Cut 1 strip 2″ × 24″ for detail on the skirt ruffle (shown in dark rose on the project doll).

2. Sew both of the dress back pieces to the dress front at the shoulders. Press the seams open and set aside.

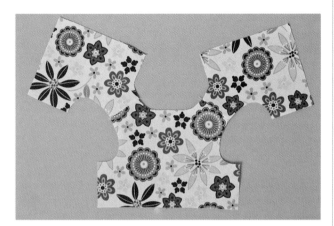

3. Sew a gathering stitch at the shoulder of each sleeve, as indicated on the sleeve pattern. With right sides together, sew a 2″ × 8″ strip of sleeve edging fabric to the bottom edge of the sleeve with a ¼″ seam allowance.

Sew sleeve edging to bottom edge of sleeve.

4. Fold under the sleeve edging so ¼″ is showing and press. Stitch across the sleeve, the same as you would for a hem.

5. With right sides together, pin the sleeves to the armhole openings, keeping the gathers at the top of the shoulders, and sew with a ¼″ seam allowance. Sew the underside of the sleeve and the dress side in a single seam. Fold under the raw edge at the back opening of the dress top ½″ and press.

Sew sleeve and dress side in single seam.

6. Fold the 2″ × 16″ strip for the neck ruffle in half, with wrong sides together, so it measures 1″ × 16″; then press. Fold under the raw edge ¼″ on each 1″ end. Sew a gathering stitch ¼″ from the 16″ raw edge. Pull the threads to gather the ruffle so it measures 7½″. Pin the ruffle to the right side of the dress at the neckline and sew. Press the ruffle so it will stand up nicely.

7. Fold the 2″ × 24″ strip for the skirt detail in half, with wrong sides together, so it measures 1″ × 24″, and press. Set aside.

8. Pin the 3″ ends of the 3″ × 45″ strip for the ruffle right sides together and sew with a ¼″ seam allowance to form a circle. Sew a ¼″ hem along one of the 45″ edges. Sew a gathering stitch along the other 45″ edge. Pull the threads to gather the ruffle so it measures 23½″.

9. Pin the 4½″ ends of the skirt rectangle right sides together and sew a ¼″ seam allowance to form a circle. Turn skirt right side out.

10. Pin the strip detail at the edge of the skirt, inserting one end into the other where the 2 ends meet. Then lay the ruffle on top of the strip detail, lining up raw edges, and pin in place. Line up the seams of the skirt, the detail strip, and the ruffle as you pin them in place. Adjust the ruffle so the gathers are evenly spaced around the skirt. Sew all 3 together with a ½" seam allowance. Press the ruffle so it will lie nicely.

Sleeve

Skirt construction

11. Sew a gathering stitch at the other edge of the skirt and pull the threads to gather the piece to about 10", so that it fits the bottom edge of the dress top. Pin the gathered skirt edge to the dress top, making sure to evenly distribute the gathers and line up the skirt seam at the center back. Slightly overlap the back opening of the dress top ¼". Sew a ½" seam around the waist.

12. Sew 2 tiny heart buttons to the dress front and 3 tiny round buttons on one side of the opening on the dress back.

13. Put the dress on the doll, over her neck. Squeeze her shoulders together to get the dress past the waistline, if you need to. Ladder stitch the dress back closed. Tie the 1"-wide ribbon around her waist. Tie the ¼"-wide ribbon around each sleeve to gather.

Dress back

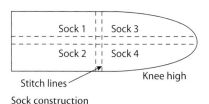

Socks

1. Turn the knee-high socks wrong side out. Sew 2 seams up the center and across the middle of the knee-high, about ½" apart.

Sock 1 | Sock 3
Sock 2 | Sock 4
Stitch lines
Knee high

Sock construction

2. Cut the toe seam off the end and then cut the knee-high in half lengthwise and widthwise. You will have 4 socks, each about 5" long.

There's no need to cut off the band at the top of the knee-high; use the band as the top of the sock. The second pair of socks won't have a band but will look equally nice. You will notice socks with and without the band on the gallery dolls. You don't need to hem the cut edge.

3. Lay each sock so the seam is in the center and then sew across the toe opening. The seam of the sock goes up the center back of the leg.

4. Turn the socks right side out. Put one pair of socks on the doll and save the other pair for your next doll.

Shoes

1. Use a pen or fine-tip marker to trace the shoe templates on the back of the vinyl. Trace 2 each of the shoe top, sole, and strap. Make center marks as shown on the template on the sole and the shoe top. Cut the pieces out carefully with a sharp pair of scissors.

2. Whipstitch the shoe tops to the shoe soles, matching up the center marks at the toes.

Shoe construction

TIP

It seems like I can never get the toe centered, so I begin sewing at the toe and around to the heel. Then I go back to the toe and sew down the other side to the heel. You will have a little extra vinyl at the heel; trim it so it overlaps just slightly and continue sewing up the heel. The pattern has extra length at the heel on purpose. Some vinyl has less give than other types of vinyl and may take a bit more to go around the shoe. It's much easier to trim a bit off at the heel than to come up short.

3. Sew a button on the rounded end of each shoe strap. Try a shoe on the doll and check for the placement of the strap. Sew the straps to the shoes at both ends. Put the shoes on the doll.

NOTE
If you match the thread color to the shoe color, the stitches will not be very noticeable. If you want the stitches to stand out, choose a contrasting thread.

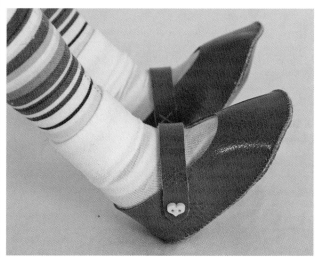

Shoes

ATTACHING THE HEAD

1. Push the neck up into the stuffing hole on the back of the head. If there is not enough room, you may need to remove some stuffing.

2. Pin the neck in place. Use a strong quilting thread and attach the head securely with a ladder stitch or invisible stitch.

ATTACHING THE HAIR

1. Use a disappearing fabric marker or straight pins to mark a circle around the head as a placement line to follow when attaching the hair. Attach the hair along this guideline and fill in the center. Notice that the hairline does not follow the seam of the neck. The top of the neck will actually be hidden by the hair.

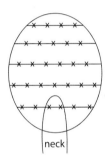

Attach hair.

2. Thread the needle (I use a curved one) with a manageable length of thread and secure the knot inside the hairline, where it will be hidden. Choose a thread color that will blend unnoticed into the hair.

3. Overlap the rows of hair like shingles. The spaces between the rows of hair are hidden by the next row of hair. Space the bundles of hair ½″ apart. Space the rows of hair ¾″ apart. Start attaching the hair at the neckline. Cut yarn in 5″ lengths for the first 3 rows and then in 3″ lengths for the top of the head. Pick up 2 strands (for a thick yarn) or 3 strands (for a thin yarn) in the center and sew to the head. If you pick up 2 strands and sew them to the head at the center of the strand, you now have 4 strands.

4. When all the hair is attached, hold the doll upside down and fluff the hair. Give her a haircut by first evening out the longest layer of hair and then snipping off any strands that seem too long.

5. Finish the doll by adding a hat or giving her a hair bow.

Emily Ann's Companion Doll

TEMPLATES REQUIRED

Find the template patterns beginning on page 106. Make templates following the instructions on page 13.

Use all the templates with an "Emily Ann's Companion Doll" label.

EMILY ANN'S COMPANION DOLL'S BODY

1. Lay out the companion doll body templates on 2 layers of body fabric, right sides together. Use a mechanical pencil to neatly trace around each template.

2. Sew around the body on the sewing line, leaving an opening at the bottom as shown on the template pattern. Cut the body out with a ⅛″ seam allowance. Turn right side out. Beginning at the hands, stuff the arms partway and then stitch across each arm. Put a small amount of stuffing in the upper arm and stitch across where the arm meets the body. Stuff the rest of the body.

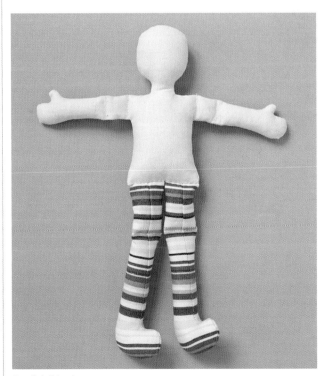

Small doll body

3. Fold the 10″ × 5½″ piece of striped fabric right sides together. Trace the leg template twice on the wrong side of the striped fabric.

4. Carefully line up the stripes and pin as you did with the large doll. Sew around the legs, leaving them open at the top for turning and stuffing.

5. Cut out with a ⅛″ seam allowance. Turn right side out.

6. Stuff the legs partway and then stitch across each leg. Put a small amount of stuffing in the top of the leg and stitch the leg closed.

7. Fold under the raw edge of the body opening, insert the legs, and pin in place. Sew across the bottom edge of the body, securing the legs.

Face

1. If you would like to add some blush to the cheeks (page 26), do it before you embroider the details.

2. Choose ¼″ snaps or buttons for the eyes. Anchor the knots at the back of the head to be hidden later by the hair. Sew the buttons on the face for eyes. Embroider the face details with embroidery floss or sewing thread. Use red or pink thread to embroider the triangle nose and give the doll a smile. Use black or brown thread for the eyelashes and eyebrows. Remember that this is Emily Ann's play doll, so the less perfect your stitches are, the better she'll look.

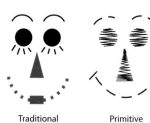

Traditional   Primitive

Embroider face.

> ### NOTE
> There are several variations in the gallery companion dolls. Two of the companion dolls have fabric triangles that are haphazardly sewn onto the face instead of the embroidered nose. You could also use a button for the nose, cut out a detail from the dress fabric, or not give the doll a nose at all. A tiny embroidered heart or French knots could be used for the mouth.

Hair

You can use the same yarn for the hair as you used for the large doll or 2 skeins of embroidery floss in a color to match the large doll. If you choose yarn, sew it to the head 1 strand at a time. If you use embroidery floss, sew it to the head 3 strands at a time.

1. Cut the yarn or floss in 2″ lengths.

2. Sew the pieces to the head in the center of the strands, using a coordinating thread. Start at the neckline and sew 4 rows of hair across the back of the head, stopping at the side seams of the head. Give the doll a haircut and a hair bow tied from ¼″-wide ribbon.

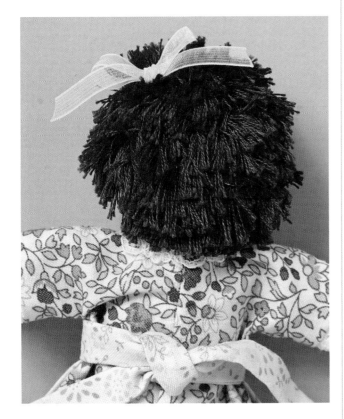

3. Sew the side seams and cut out with a ¼" seam allowance. Turn the pantaloons right side out.

4. Fold under ¼" at the raw edge at the waist. Use floss or quilting thread to make a running stitch around the waist, beginning and ending at the center front. Put the pantaloons on the doll. Pull the floss at the waist to gather and tie in a knot.

Dressing the Companion Doll

These clothes are tiny, but using the trace, sew, and cut technique will make quick work of dressing this doll.

Pantaloons

1. Pin 2 squares 5" × 5" of pantaloon fabric with right sides together. Trace the companion doll pantaloon template with a pencil. Cut across the top of the fabric on the waistline and across the bottom edge of the fabric on the pantaloon legs.

2. Sew around the inside of the legs and crotch in a single seam. Open the legs and sew a 4" piece of ½"-wide trim to the bottom edge of each leg and then press.

Make pantaloons.

Dress

1. Fold the dress fabric with right sides together. Pin the fabric together and trace the dress template on the wrong side of the fabric with the top edge of the sleeves on the fold. Cut the neck hole, sleeve edge, and bottom edge of the dress on the traced lines. Cut an opening at the center on the back of the dress as shown on the template pattern. Just as you did with the pantaloons, add the sleeve trim before sewing the sleeves and side seams.

Sew seam and attach trim.

2. Open up the dress and sew a 4″ piece of ½″-wide trim around the right side of each sleeve on the pencil line and press under.

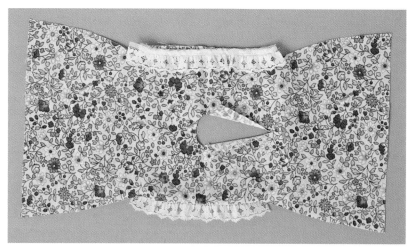

Prepare dress piece.

3. With right sides together, pin the dress together, matching the sleeves, the neck, and the dress bottom edge. Sew the underside of the sleeve and the dress side in a single seam. Cut out the sides of the dress with a ¼″ seam allowance. Sew a ¼″ hem at the bottom of the dress. Turn the dress right side out. Sew a 4″ piece of ½″-wide trim around the neckline. Add a tiny heart button to the center front of the dress at the neckline. Put the dress on the doll and use a ladder stitch to close the back of the dress.

Construct dress.

Apron

1. Cut a 3″ × 6″ rectangle from the ruffle fabric for the apron and a 1½″ × 20″ strip for the tie. Hem the apron on both 3″ sides and 1 of the 6″ sides. An option would be to use ribbon in place of the tie.

2. Sew a gathering stitch on the 6″ side that is not hemmed. Pull the gathering stitch so the apron measures 3″ wide. With right sides together, pin the tie to the apron on the gathered edge, matching up the centers. Attach the tie with a ¼″ seam allowance across the top of the apron. Fold the raw edges of the tie under and press. Sew a seam down the length of the tie.

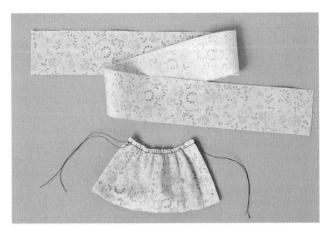

Apron construction

3. Put the apron on the doll and tie at the back. The only thing left is to decide where you'll display her.

Front of small doll

Back of small doll

RAG DOLLS

This doll is wonderful no matter what your color choices are.

For a more traditional look, choose a red, white, and blue color palette. Check out some of the retro fabrics for a twist on the usual. If you want your doll to look old or worn, don't use bright-colored fabrics. Instead of white for the socks, pantaloons, or apron, choose an off-white. Stay away from prints that have stark white backgrounds. You could also make the doll with leftover fabric from the quilt you just made. She could be soft and sweet or loud and colorful. You could also choose dots instead of stripes for the legs. The choices are endless. The rag dolls shown in the gallery were all made with the Emily Ann pattern. Each one was made with different color combinations, and some trims were added or omitted.

Betty Ann

Lizzy Ann

Lacey Ann

Connie Ann

Patty Ann

Jenny Ann

Rachel Ann

Template Patterns

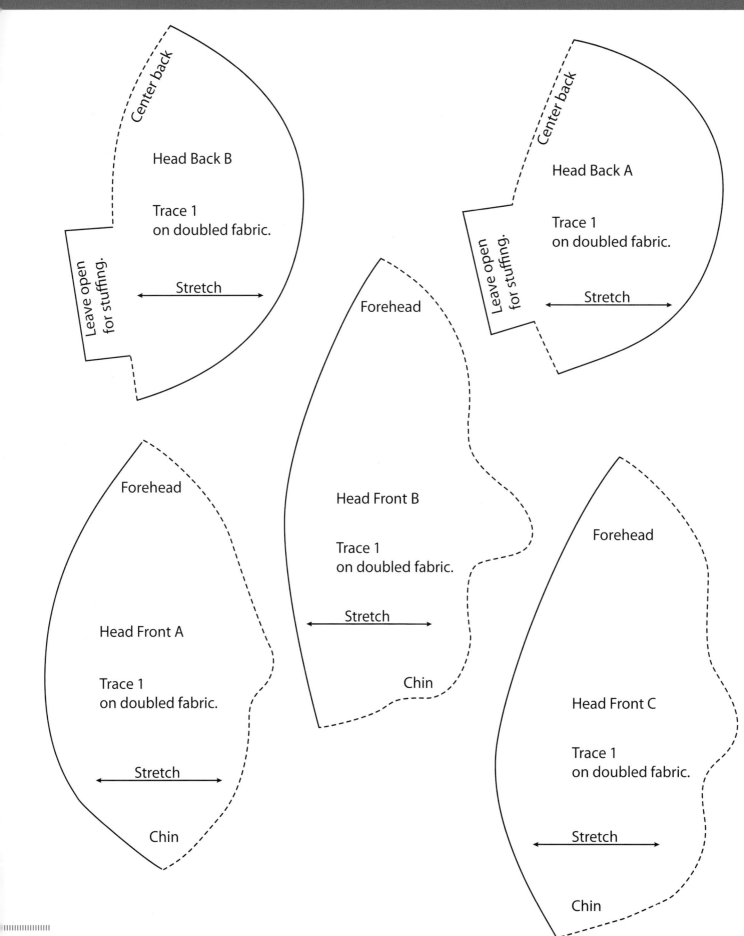

Center back

Head Back B

Trace 1
on doubled fabric.

Stretch

Leave open
for stuffing.

Center back

Head Back A

Trace 1
on doubled fabric.

Stretch

Leave open
for stuffing.

Forehead

Head Front A

Trace 1
on doubled fabric.

Stretch

Chin

Forehead

Head Front B

Trace 1
on doubled fabric.

Stretch

Chin

Forehead

Head Front C

Trace 1
on doubled fabric.

Stretch

Chin

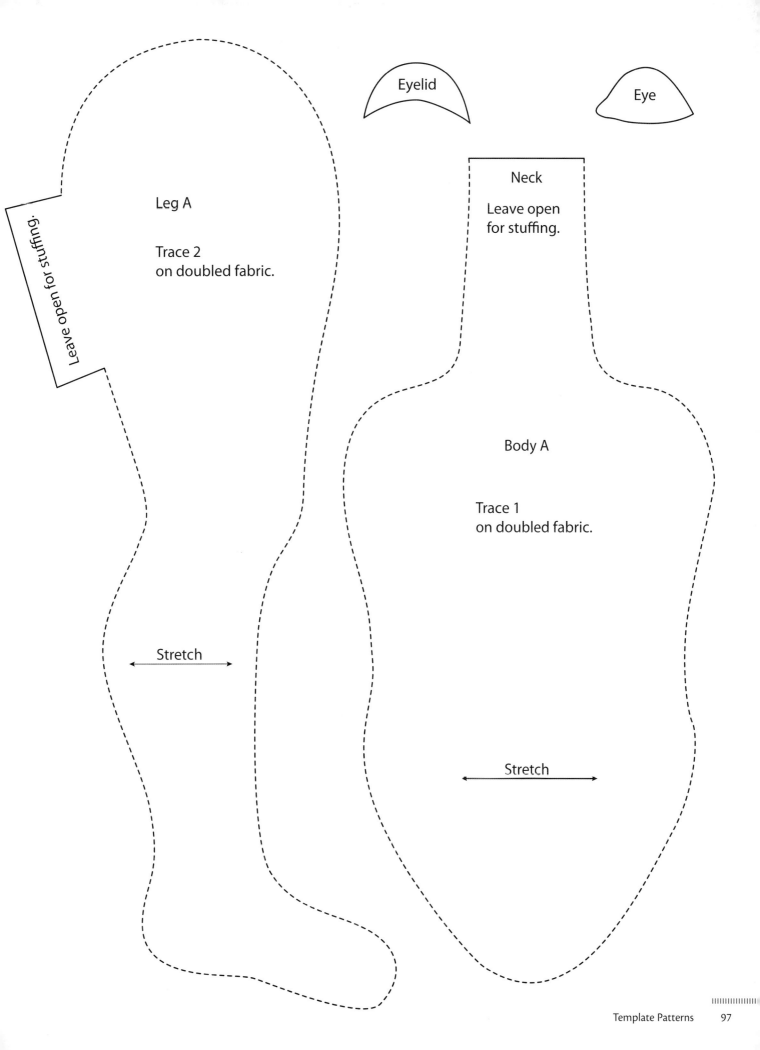

Eyelid

Eye

Leg A

Trace 2
on doubled fabric.

Leave open for stuffing.

Neck

Leave open
for stuffing.

Body A

Trace 1
on doubled fabric.

Stretch

Stretch

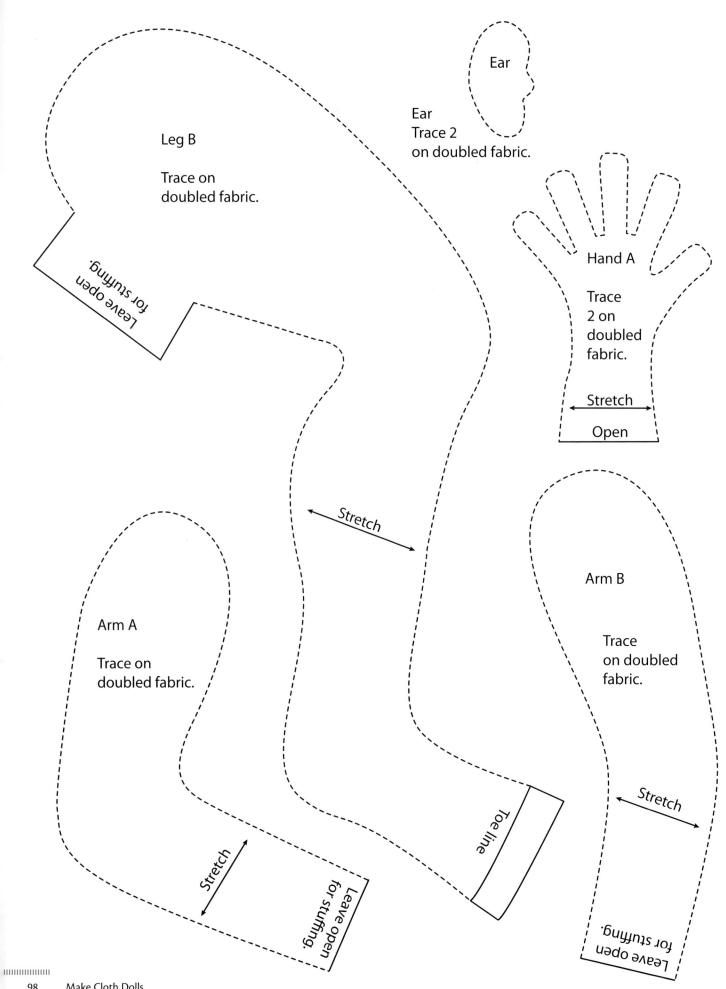

Ear

Ear
Trace 2
on doubled fabric.

Leg B

Trace on
doubled fabric.

Leave open for stuffing.

Hand A

Trace
2 on
doubled
fabric.

Stretch

Open

Stretch

Arm A

Trace on
doubled fabric.

Arm B

Trace
on doubled
fabric.

Stretch

Stretch

Leave open for stuffing.

Toe line

Leave open for stuffing.

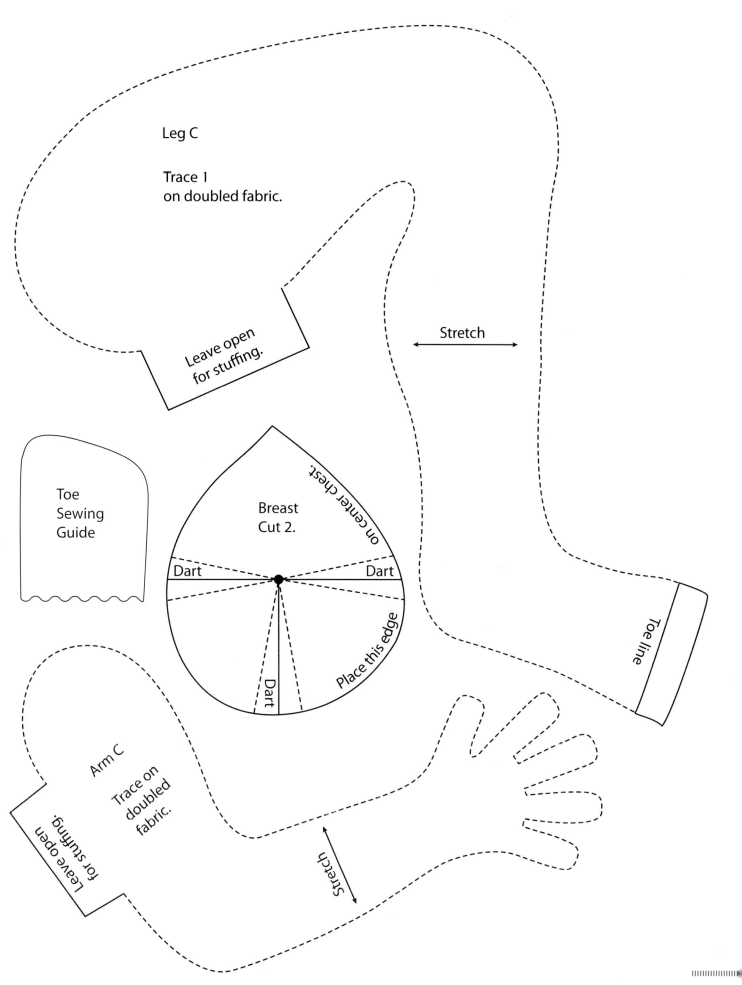

Leg C

Trace 1
on doubled fabric.

Leave open
for stuffing.

Stretch

Toe
Sewing
Guide

Breast
Cut 2.

on center chest.

Dart   Dart

Place this edge

Dart

Toe line

Arm C

Trace on
doubled
fabric.

Leave open
for stuffing.

Stretch

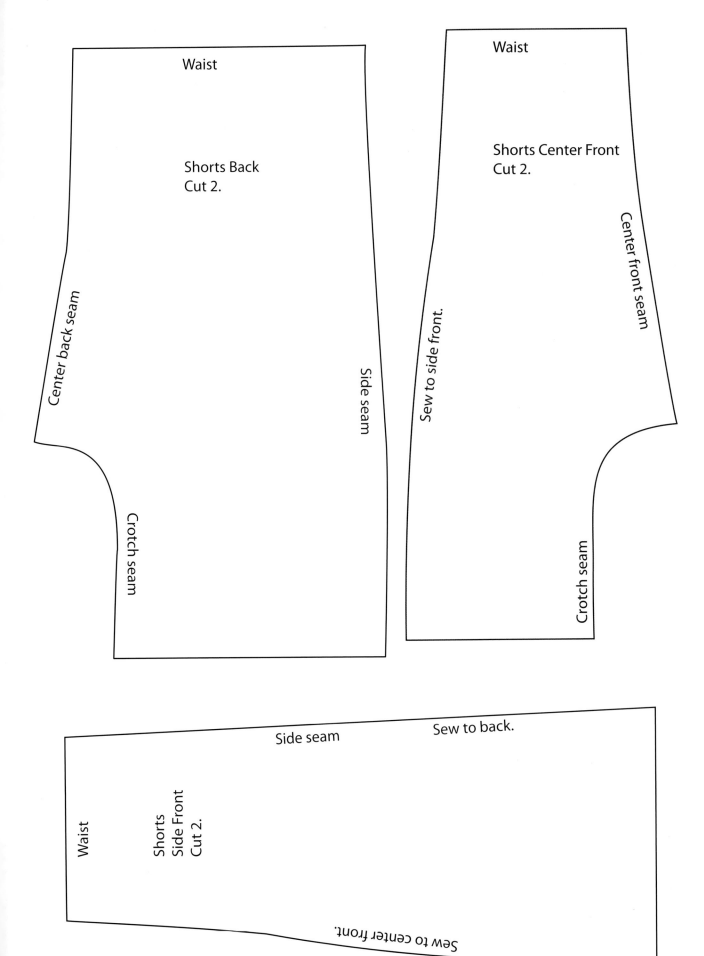

Waist

Shorts Back
Cut 2.

Center back seam

Crotch seam

Side seam

Waist

Shorts Center Front
Cut 2.

Sew to side front.

Center front seam

Crotch seam

Side seam

Sew to back.

Waist

Shorts
Side Front
Cut 2.

Sew to center front.

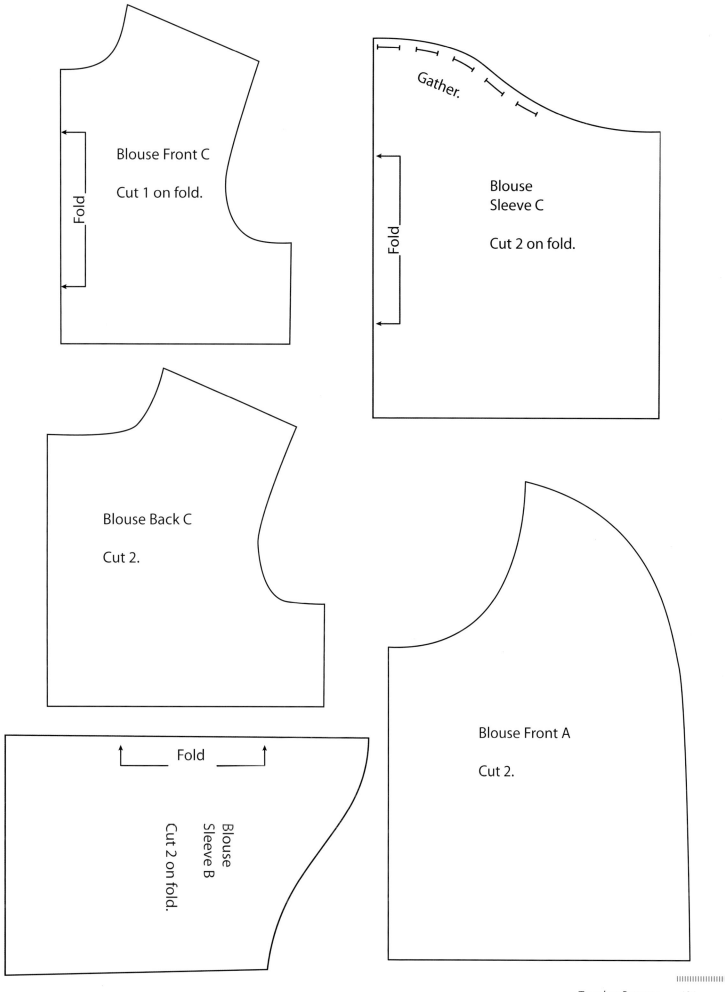

Blouse Front C

Cut 1 on fold.

Fold

Gather.

Blouse
Sleeve C

Cut 2 on fold.

Fold

Blouse Back C

Cut 2.

Fold

Blouse
Sleeve B
Cut 2 on fold.

Blouse Front A

Cut 2.

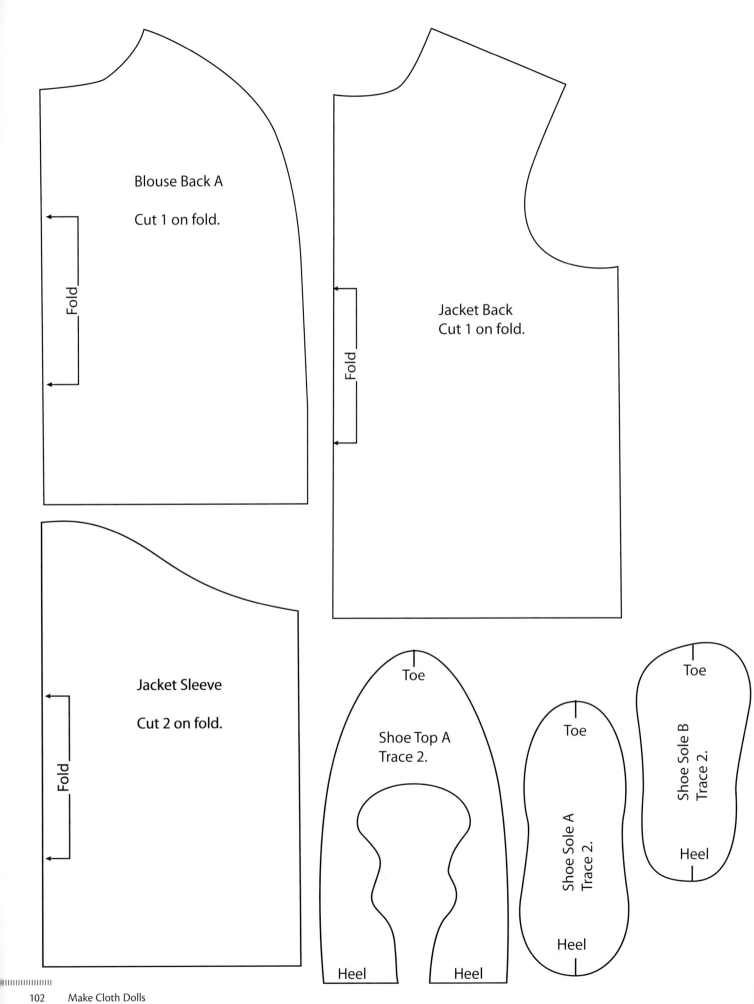

Blouse Back A

Cut 1 on fold.

Fold

Jacket Back
Cut 1 on fold.

Fold

Jacket Sleeve

Cut 2 on fold.

Fold

Toe

Shoe Top A
Trace 2.

Heel

Heel

Toe

Shoe Sole A
Trace 2.

Heel

Toe

Shoe Sole B
Trace 2.

Heel

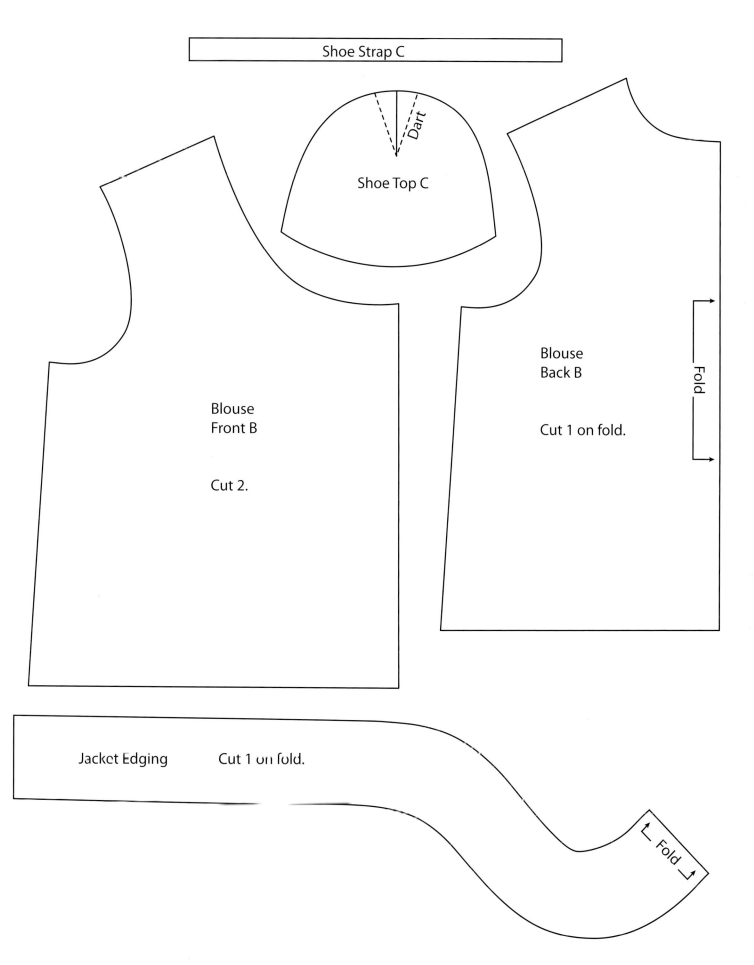

Shoe Strap C

Shoe Top C

Dart

Blouse
Front B

Cut 2.

Blouse
Back B

Cut 1 on fold.

Fold

Jacket Edging   Cut 1 on fold.

Fold

Jacket Front
Cut 2.

Shopping Bag

Cut out on solid lines.

Fold on dashed lines.

Scrapbooking
Supplies

Cut out on solid lines.

Fold on dashed lines.

Emily Ann

Emily Ann Shoe Strap   Cut 2.

Shoe Top
Cut 2.

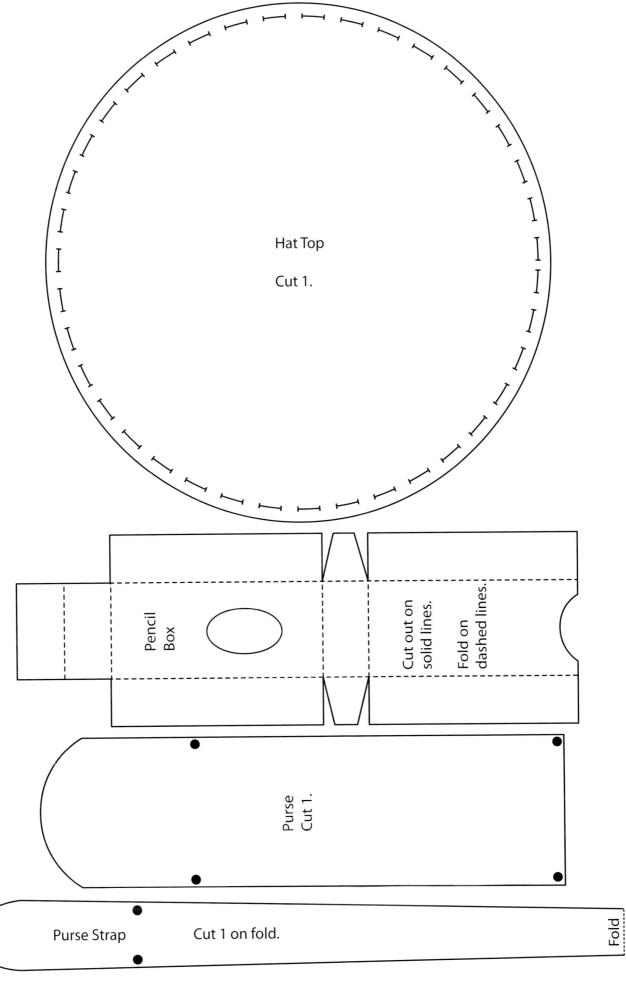

Hat Top

Cut 1.

Pencil
Box

Cut out on
solid lines.

Fold on
dashed lines.

Purse
Cut 1.

Purse Strap   Cut 1 on fold.

Fold

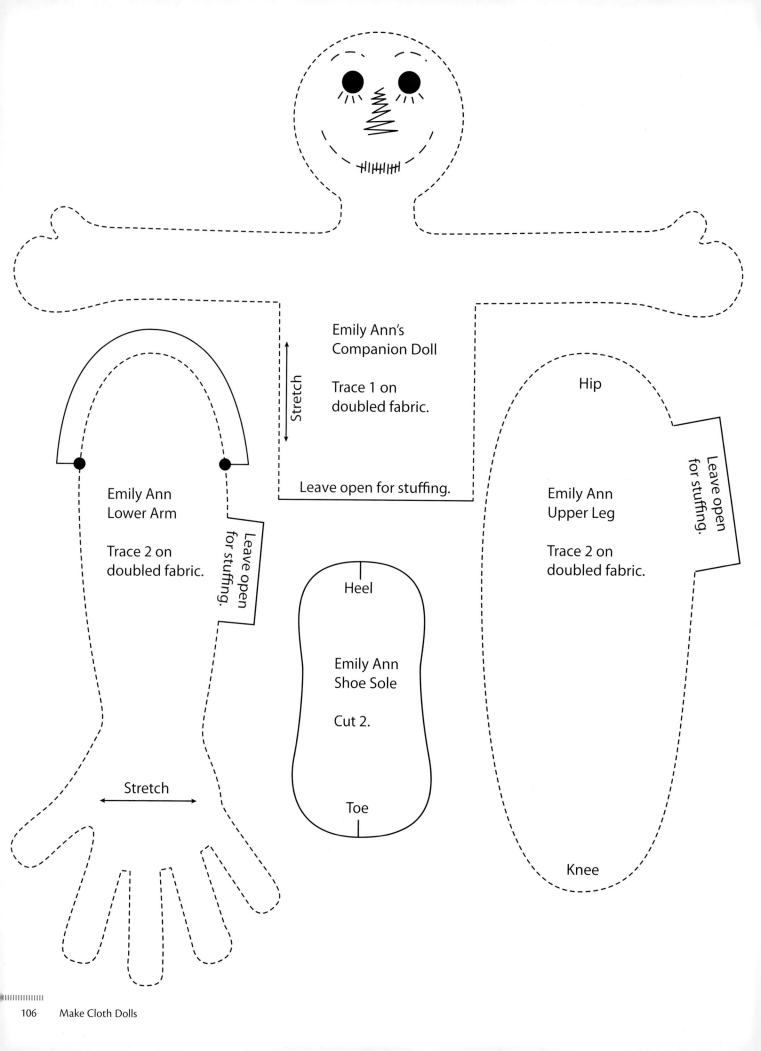

Emily Ann's
Companion Doll

Trace 1 on
doubled fabric.

Stretch

Leave open for stuffing.

Emily Ann
Lower Arm

Trace 2 on
doubled fabric.

Leave open for stuffing.

Stretch

Hip

Leave open for stuffing.

Emily Ann
Upper Leg

Trace 2 on
doubled fabric.

Heel

Emily Ann
Shoe Sole

Cut 2.

Toe

Knee

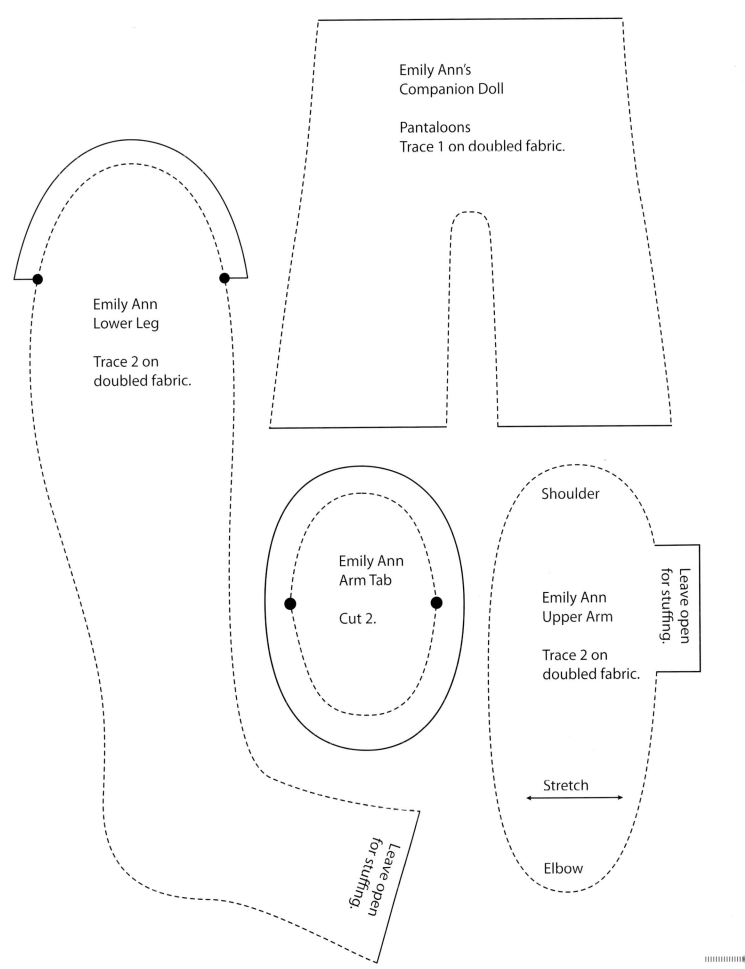

Emily Ann's
Companion Doll

Pantaloons
Trace 1 on doubled fabric.

Emily Ann
Lower Leg

Trace 2 on
doubled fabric.

Emily Ann
Arm Tab

Cut 2.

Shoulder

Leave open
for stuffing.

Emily Ann
Upper Arm

Trace 2 on
doubled fabric.

Stretch

Elbow

Leave open
for stuffing.

Leave open
for stuffing.

Emily Ann
Leg Tab

Cut 2.

Emily Ann
Body Front and Back

Trace 1 on
doubled fabric.

Trace, sew, then cut out.

Forehead

Emily Ann
Head Front

Trace 1 on
doubled fabric.

Stretch

Chin

Stretch

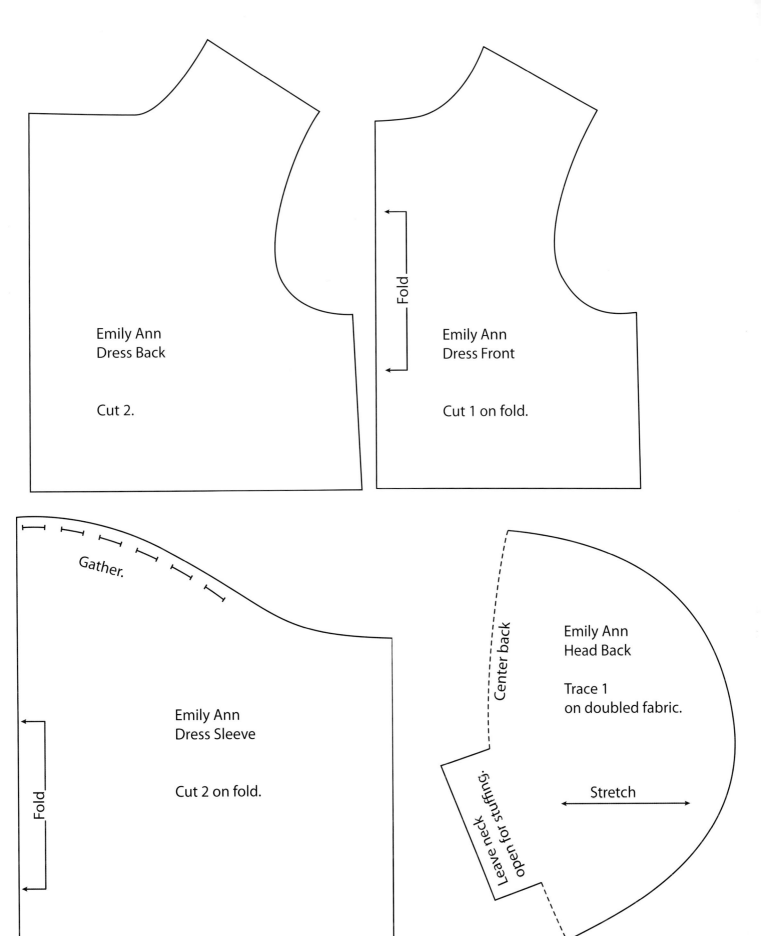

Emily Ann
Dress Back

Cut 2.

Fold

Emily Ann
Dress Front

Cut 1 on fold.

Gather.

Fold

Emily Ann
Dress Sleeve

Cut 2 on fold.

Center back

Leave neck
open for stuffing.

Emily Ann
Head Back

Trace 1
on doubled fabric.

Stretch

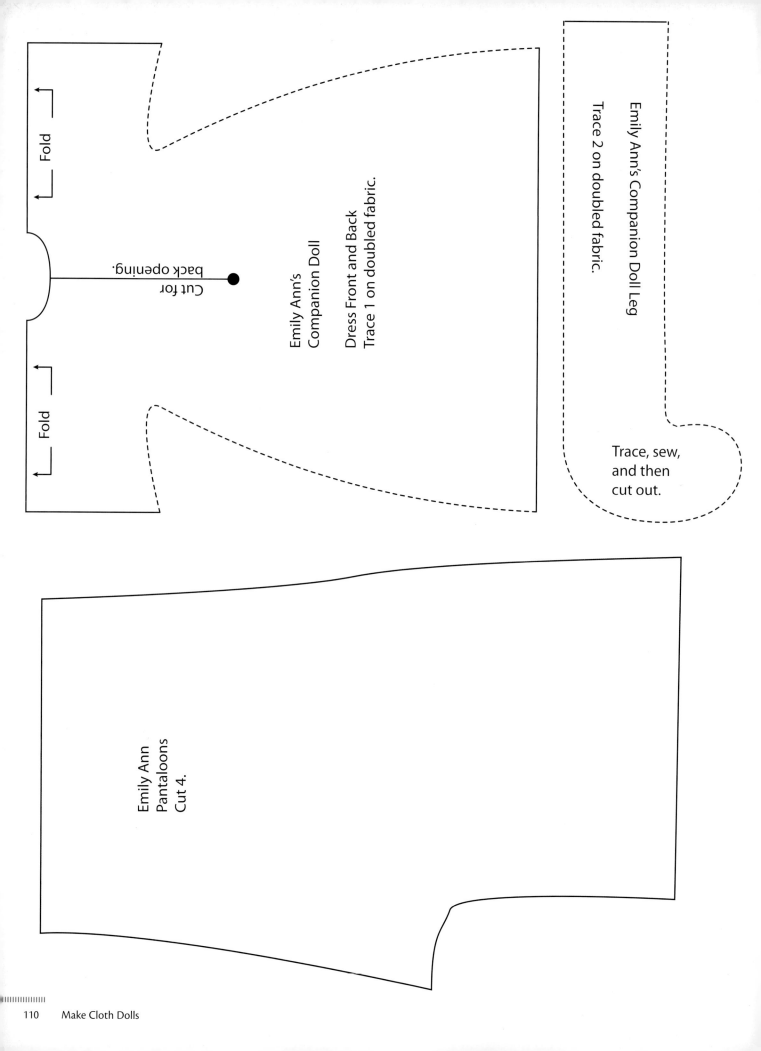

Fold

Fold

Cut for
back opening.

Emily Ann's
Companion Doll

Dress Front and Back
Trace 1 on doubled fabric.

Emily Ann's Companion Doll Leg

Trace 2 on doubled fabric.

Trace, sew,
and then
cut out.

Emily Ann
Pantaloons
Cut 4.

Resources

Quilting supplies, Liquitex paint products, Alex Anderson's 4-in-1 Essential Sewing Tool

Cotton Patch

www.quiltusa.com

Turning Tubes

Terese Cato

www.teresecato.com

Small buttons, themed buttons

Jesse James Beads

www.dressitup.com

Shoelace yarn

YLI

www.ylicorp.com

Yarn

Lion Brand Yarn

www.lionbrand.com

Fabric (Check websites for a store near you.)

Timeless Treasures Fabrics

www.ttfabrics.com

Robert Kaufman Co. Fabrics

www.robertkaufman.com

P&B Textiles

www.pbtex.com

About the Author

When I was 11 years old, my Aunt Marie taught me how to sew, knit, and crochet. Money was scarce when she was young, so her mother made all her clothes. When Marie got a little older, her mother taught her to sew for herself. There were never any store-bought patterns. Her mother taught her to make her own patterns with a marker and a stack of newspapers.

As I think back on it now, I'm sure that if I had been a bit older I would have told Aunt Marie it was too hard. As young as I was, I listened and followed her directions. Marie had no formal training, only the skills learned from her mother. She taught me how clothes were constructed, and I learned to make patterns with a marker and a stack of newspapers. When I ran out of fabric, I started looking in my brother's closet for things he wouldn't miss.

I think about Aunt Marie all the time when I'm sewing. It is that "I can do that!" attitude that she instilled in me that has allowed me to paint, weave, and do woodworking and woodcarving. I have been sewing for 38 years now, and I still pull out the newspaper when I have an idea for a new project.

Please visit my website: www.teresecato.com

Great Titles *from* C&T PUBLISHING

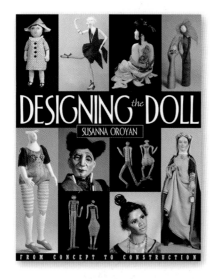

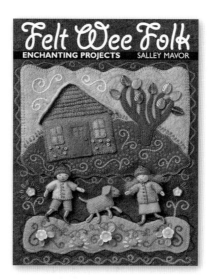

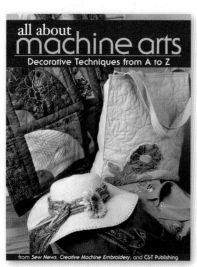

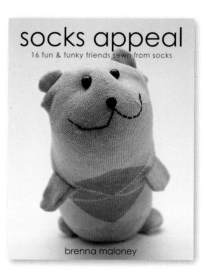

Available at your local retailer or **www.ctpub.com** *or* **800-284-1114**

For a list of other fine books from C&T Publishing, visit our website to view our catalog online:

C&T PUBLISHING, INC.

P.O. Box 1456
Lafayette, CA 94549
800-284-1114

Email: ctinfo@ctpub.com
Website: www.ctpub.com

C&T Publishing's professional photography services are now available to the public. Visit us at www.ctmediaservices.com.

Tips and Techniques can be found at www.ctpub.com > Consumer Resources > Quiltmaking Basics: Tips & Techniques for Quiltmaking & More

For sewng supplies:

COTTON PATCH

1025 Brown Ave.
Lafayette, CA 94549
Store: 925-284-1177
Mail order: 925-283-7883

Email: CottonPa@aol.com
Website: www.quiltusa.com

Note: Fabrics used in the projects shown may not be currently available, as fabric manufacturers keep most fabrics in print for only a short time.